P9-CJM-508

COMEDIANS

COMEDIANS

by

TREVOR
GRIFFITHS

Grove Press, Inc., New York

ISBN: 0-394-17913-7
Grove Press ISBN: 0-8021-4009-2

Library of Congress Catalog Card Number: 76-16727

First Evergreen Edition 1976

First Printing 1976

Distributed by Random House, Inc., New York

GROVE PRESS, INC., 196 West Houston Street, New York, N.Y. 10014

The first performance in Great Britain of *Comedians* was given at the Nottingham Playhouse on 20th February 1975. It was directed by Richard Eyre, and the décor was by John Gunter. The cast was as follows:

GED MURRAY	Dave Hill
MR. PATEL	Talat Hussain
EDDIE WATERS	Jimmy Jewel
CLUB SECRETARY	John Joyce
BERT CHALLENOR	Ralph Nossek
GETHIN PRICE	Jonathan Pryce
SAMMY SAMUELS	Louis Raynes
GEORGE MCBRAIN	Stephen Rea
CARETAKER	Richard Simpson
PHIL MURRAY	James Warrior
MICK CONNOR	Tom Wilkinson

ACT ONE

A classroom in a secondary school in Manchester, about three miles east of the centre, on the way to Ashton-under-Lyne and the hills of east Lancashire. Built 1947 in the now disappearing but still familiar two-storey style, the school doubles as evening centre for the area, and will half-fill as the evening progresses, with the followers of yoga, karate, cordon bleu cookery, 'O' level English, secretarial prelims, do-it-yourself, small investments and antique furniture. Adults will return to school and the school will do its sullen best to accommodate them.

This room, on the ground floor, is smallish, about a dozen chipped and fraying desks, two dozen chairs set out in rows facing the small dais on which stands the teacher's desk, with green blackboard unwiped from the day's last stand beyond. Two starkish lights, on the window side of the room, are on, flintily, lighting about a third of it. A clock (real: keeping real time for the evening) over the board says 7.27. Cupboards of haphazard heights and styles line the walls, above which the dogged maps, charts, tables, illustrations and notices warp, fray, tear, curl and droop their way to limbo. Windows on the left wall show the night dark and wet.

The SCHOOL CARETAKER, *old, gnarled, tiny, is up on a small ladder trying to sponge recent graffiti from the blackboard, in the lit segment of the room. He has done away with the 'F' fairly successfully and now begins on the 'U'. C,K,O,F,F,N,O,B,H,O,L,E stretch out before him. He mutters 'Dirty bastards, filthy fuckers' as he sponges.*

GETHIN PRICE *arrives, in wet raincoat, carrying a long canvas bag and a pint of hot water. He puts down bag and mug by a desk, removes*

7

coat and shirt, takes shaving tackle from the bag and sits, in his greying vest, to shave in the tiny mirror he has propped before him. PRICE *wears a flat Lenin-like cloth or denim hat, which he leaves on.*

Corridor sounds, as people hurry for their classes. PRICE *shaves with deft precision, surprisingly dainty-handed.*

The CARETAKER *finishes, descends, catches sight of* PRICE, *almost falls the final step to the floor.*

CARETAKER: Are you in here?

> (PRICE *looks round, behind, about, with strange clown-like timing, the foam gleaming like a mask, brush poised.*)

PRICE (*finally*): Yeah.

> (*The* CARETAKER *sniffs, looks for his clipboard and list of classes; scans it.*)

CARETAKER: I don't see it.

PRICE: Been here since January. (*Pause.*) Mr. Waters . . .

CARETAKER: Waters. Oh, him. (*Studying* PRICE *at his ablutions.*) What is it, Gents' Hairdressing?

PRICE: Yeah. Some'at like that.

CARETAKER: I thought you practised on balloons. I saw it once in a film . . .

> (CARETAKER *stumps out, carrying the ladder, pins* PHIL MURRAY *to the door as they pass.* MURRAY *in. Stops in doorway as he sees* PRICE's *foaming white face.*)

PHIL (*sour, his dominant note*): Jesus, is it Christmas already.

> (PRICE *shaves on, smiling briefly.* MURRAY *carries his two suit-cases to a desk and deposits them tidily before sitting down. He's twenty-nine, small, dapper, an insurance agent in thick-fitting dark three-piece suit.*)

Christ, what a flap. God knows where that bloody idiot of a brother of mine's got to. (*He checks his watch against the clock.*) He's probably forgot, the stupid mare. Be having a game o'bones in the New Inn. (*Across to* PRICE.) Are you ready then? (PRICE *grunts yes or no, it makes no matter.*) *I* am. By God, I am. I've worked meself puce for tonight. I have. I have that. And if that dozy prick . . .

> (*He leaves it hanging, minatory.* GEORGE MCBRAIN *in, straight from work. He's a docker, big, beefy, wears an old parka,*

8

*jeans, boots, shock of black hair, extrovert Ulsterman in his late
thirties.*)

MCBRAIN (*arms wide in doorway*): De Da!
(*Nothing. He looks from* MURRAY *to* PRICE.)
Well, I found the stones, now all I've gotta do is find
the classroom. (*Advancing, bag in hand.*) Are we all ready
then? Tonight you will see . . . something! Overtime every
night this week but am I worried? Not a bit of it. Because
I have what it takes. And when you have it . . . (*He produces
a can of Worthington 'E' from his bag on the desk.*) . . . by
God you have it!

PHIL (*to* PRICE): He sounds as if he's had it for a while too.

MCBRAIN: Mock on, brother. I can forgive your jealousy.

PHIL: You get more like that Paisley every day, George——

MCBRAIN (*Paisley at once*): Mock not the reverend doctor, Mr.
Murray. There's not many left of us can walk on water.
(PRICE *finishes, replaces shaving tackle, begins to dress.*)
How's it going then, Geth?

PRICE: OK.
(*He picks up the mug. Leaves the room.* MCBRAIN *slowly follows
him half-way, stops, looks at* PHIL MURRAY.)

MCBRAIN: Feeling the strain, doubtless.

PHIL (*trying a shiny pair of black pointed shoes on*): Teacher's pet?
He's just a moody bugger.

MCBRAIN: Where's your kid, then? And where's the bloody rest
of 'em? Look at the time . . .

PHIL: Don't ask me about our kid. It's bad enough I have to
work with him. I was picking him up on Market Street
wasn't I, seven o'clock. *I* was there. Parked on a double
yellow line wasn't I? If he'd been there, there'd've been two
of us.
(SAMMY SAMUELS *and* MICK CONNOR *in.* SAMUELS, *forty-one,
fat, Manchester Jewish, cigar, heavy finely cut black overcoat,
homburg, white silk scarf, black attaché case, first in.*)

MCBRAIN (*Stan Laurel voice*): Hi, Olly.

SAMUELS (*evenly*): Piss off.
(*He crosses to a desk, carefully removes hat, coat (which he
shakes), scarf, and adjusts his shirt cuffs so that the diamond*

9

cufflinks do their work below the sleeve of his good wool suit.
CONNOR *stands in the doorway, rain dripping from his donkey jacket, beneath which we glimpse hired evening dress and crumpled buttonhole.*)

MCBRAIN: Oh, Christ.

CONNOR: Almost, my son. Try again.

MCBRAIN: You're drowned. What've you come in your gear for?

CONNOR: Laid off again. Thought I'd get it done with. Bloody weather. No pigging buses.

PHIL: You'll look like a dog's dinner.

MCBRAIN (*an explosion*): The Kennomeat Kid. Ha! That's good that! I like that! (*Frank Carson voice.*) It's the way I tell 'em.
(*The groans of the others increase his glee.*)

SAMUELS (*strong Manchester accent, occasional Jewish nasality*): These pipes are hot, Mick. Get over here and dry out.
(CONNOR *crosses to the pipes. We see 'Wimpey' on the PVC patch on the back of the jacket as he removes it.*)
(*Seeing the suit jacket*): Hey, that's not a bad fit. Where'd you gerrit, Woolworth's?

CONNOR: S'matter of fact belonged to a feller I know passed on.

SAMUELS: Not surprised wearing a suit like that.

CONNOR: What's wrong with the suit? It's a bit wet . . .

SAMUELS: S'hard to put your finger on . . .

MCBRAIN: . . . as the actress said to the bishop . . .
(*Groan.*)

SAMUELS (*studiously contemptuous of the interruption*): It's the sort of suit you walk into a tailor's in and ask for the cheapest suit in the shop and he says you're wearing it. (*Groan.*) Don't groan, you scum, learn.

CONNOR (*studying the suit*): S'been a good suit.

SAMUELS: It was doomed the moment it left the animal. Believe me, I know about these things.

PHIL: Christ, he's doing half his bloody act . . .

SAMUELS: Don't worry about me, old son. Plenty more where that came from.

MCBRAIN: Right. Why should Ken Dodd worry about some obscure Manchester Jew nicking his lines? Ha!

(SAMUELS *smiles, a little frost around the teeth, at* MCBRAIN.)

SAMUELS: Why indeed. Why indeed.

CONNOR (*aware of that faint crackle*): Sure it's a detail. A detail it is.

MCBRAIN (*in* WATERS's *exact voice, assuming his manner*): Ah, but detail, friend, is all. Think on now.

(EDDIE WATERS *in, quick, purposeful, behind* SAMUELS's *back.*)

SAMUELS: Where *is* His Grace, by the way . . .?

WATERS: He's here.

(*There's a small but discernible reaction in the others, a regression to childhood responses.*)

(*Already within reach of his desk.*) Sorry it's late. I had to check the equipment down at the club. No piano. (*Bloody hells of concern.*) It's all right, they've had one sent down from Edge Lane. (*Pause.*) Right, let's get cracking, we haven't got all night. (*He's deposited his gear around the desk, papers, books, a stop watch, other materials and equipment.*) Get the tables sorted and settle down while I take a leak . . .

(*He's on his way to the door. The others break and begin drawing the desks and chairs into roughly parallel sides of a hollow square. In the doorway he meets* PRICE, *returning.* PRICE *has removed his hat to reveal an almost wholly shaven skull, the hair dense and metallic on the scalp.*)

(*Stopping, staring.*) Mr. Price. (*Over shoulder, very dry.*) Less noise if you would, gentlemen. There may be people trying to sleep in other classrooms. (*Back to* PRICE *now, staring at head.*) All . . . ready?

PRICE: Yeah. Just about, Mr. Waters.

WATERS (*the head incomprehensible yet unmentionable*): Still finishing on the song . . .?

PRICE: I'm not doing a song.

WATERS: How d'you mean? How're you gonna get off?

PRICE (*evasive, stubborn*): I've er . . . I've bin working on some'at else.

WATERS (*some faint concern*): Since when?

PRICE: Oh, last week. I dint like the act. I found some'at in the book you lent us.

11

WATERS: Yes, but you've not changed the basic . . . I mean a
week . . .

PRICE (*breaking deliberately into the room*): It'll be all right, Mr.
Waters.

(*He takes a desk end with* PHIL. WATERS *watches him, leaves.*)

MCBRAIN (*to* PRICE): Hey. (PRICE *looks at him over his shoulder.*)
Love the hairdo.

PRICE (*evenly*): Nice, innit.

SAMUELS: Reminds me of a girl I used to know. (*Reflective.*) I've
known some funny women.

MCBRAIN: Reminds me of the wife. After the operation.

CONNOR: She's had it as well has she?

MCBRAIN: Ey, eh . . .

(*They square up to each other in mock battle stances.*)

PHIL: Are you shifting these desks or what?

MCBRAIN: I heard the Church had granted the Pope a special
dispensation . . . to become a nun.

(*Beat.*)

CONNOR: That's right. Only on Fridays though.

(*They grin, begin humping a desk.*)

PHIL: Look at the bloody time. I'll cut his legs off.

SAMUELS: And he'll still be bigger than you.

(PRICE *has taken a tiny violin and large bow from his bag,
begins to tune it quietly.*)

MCBRAIN: What the *hell's* that thing?

PRICE (*as to a child, slowly*): This? It's a . . . very, very small . . .
violin. Vi. O. Lin. Try it. Vio. Lin.

MCBRAIN: Vio. Nil. Vay. Lone. Velo. Line. No. Velo. No . . .

PRICE: Vio. Lin. Keep practising. It'll come.

(MCBRAIN *stands blinking, trying to say the word.*)

SAMUELS: Hey. Vic Oliver. You're never Jewish.

PRICE (*perfect Manchester Jewish*): You wanna make some kind of
a bet, Moses?

MCBRAIN (*elated*): Violin! Got it! Vionole, shit!

(WATERS *back in. They sit down at their desks with a muffled
clatter and scrape.*)

WATERS: Right, let's see who's here . . . Jack Thomas is out.
Tonsilitis.

MCBRAIN: Tough. Poor old Jack.

WATERS: What about your brother, Mr. Murray?

PHIL (*nervous*): He'll be here, Mr. Waters. He's probably been held up somewhere.

SAMUELS: Likely he got a bit behind with his milk-round.

CONNOR: I've heard tell it's more than behind these milkmen are after getting. Sure my wife's the only woman in the street ours hasn't parked his float in.

(*Beat.*)

CONNOR ⎱ :
MCBRAIN ⎰ : The stuck-up bitch!
SAMUELS ⎰ :

(*Laughter.*)

WATERS (*dry*): Oh, we're working tonight, gentlemen. How can they say Music Hall is dead when jokes like that survive . . . down the ages? Right, settle down, we'll make a start. (*Looking at clock.*) Now, we're down at Grey Mare Lane at eight thirty-five or so for a nine o'clock start. That gives us till about twenty-five past. And remember we come back here as soon as it's finished, just to round things off and er . . . listen to the verdict. Which brings me to the man they're sending. (*Taking opened envelope from inside pocket, taking letter out.*) His name's . . . Bert Challenor . . . some of you may have heard of him . . . he worked Number Ones a fair while way back, before he took up . . . talent-spotting. He'll be here back side of eight, so you'll get a chance to weigh him up before the off. (*Pause. Scanning them.*) I don't want to say much about him. He's an agents' man. Which means he has power. I'd better say this, though: I've never rated him. And he doesn't reckon much to me either.

CONNOR: Sounds a nice chap.

WATERS: Now I'm not saying any of this is going to count against you. But we . . . have our differences. I'd hoped for someone else, to tell the truth.

(*Puzzled looks, faint consternation.*)

SAMUELS: How do you mean, differences?

WATERS: I don't wanna spend all night on it . . . I never joined

13

his . . . Comedy Artists and Managers Federation, for a
kick-off. They took it bad, for some reason. I didn't like
what they stood for. I've been a union man all my life, it
wasn't that. . . . They wanted the market. . . . They wanted
to control entry into the game. I told 'em no comedian (*odd,
particular emphasis*) worth his salt could ever 'federate' with
a manager. (*Pause, sniff.*) And as far as I'm concerned no
comedian ever did . . .

PRICE (*very distinctly*): You think he'd . . . fail us . . . just for
that, Mr. Waters, do you?

WATERS: That's not what I said . . .

MCBRAIN: Nobody'll fail me. I'm unfailable.

CONNOR: Hark at the Pope, now.

PRICE (*piercing, within the control*): Well, what then?

WATERS: Well, put baldly, if I've done a job with you lot, he'll
see it, and he won't like it. That's all.
(*They look at each other, a trifle more concerned.*)

MCBRAIN (*reassuring*): What does it matter, a comic's a comic.

SAMUELS: Not in Rabbi Challenor's book he ain't.

WATERS (*deliberate*): Not in Eddie Waters' book either.
(*Silence. Some sniffs.*)
I probably overstate the problem. You're all good enough
. . . now . . . to force his hand, without playing down . . .

MCBRAIN: Crème de la crème.

SAMUELS: A little clotted here and there perhaps.

MCBRAIN: More there than here, Isaac.

PRICE: Why don't we start?

OTHERS (*repeat*): Why don't we start? Why don't we start?
(*Rather crazily to each other, begin to discuss it.*)
What an excellent suggestion, give that man a balaclava for
his pains . . .

WATERS: All right. In the time remaining I thought we might
just run through a few exercises to get the blood running . . .
(GED MURRAY *half backs into the room, soaked through. He's
large, gentle, direct, open, very far from stupid. Pale, with
bad teeth and balding. He wears a milkman's brown coat and
hat. He continues, a line at a time, as he makes his way into
the room, greets people with winks or smiles, finds his chair,*

14

adjusts it, sits down, apparently wholly unaware of the interruption of process he represents. A brilliant comic performance, in other words.)

GED (*taking coat off, shaking it, adjusting himself*): Sorry I'm late. It's bloody pissing down out there. I fell asleep on the settee watching *Crossroads*. So I had to nip down t'depot and borrow a float to get here. And t'bloody battery were flat. Got stuck on the Old Road. Walked the last sodding mile. Evening, Mr. Waters. (*He hits his seat next to brother* PHIL.) Evening, all. (*A big friendly grin.*)

ALL (*in chorus*): Good evening, Mr. Woodentop.

(WATERS *waits, a little impatient, for quiet.*)

PHIL (*hoarse, hostile*): I waited ten minutes on a double yellow line . . .

GED (*easily*): Don't worry, I'm here now.

PHIL: Couldn't you have put some'at else on?

GED: What's wrong with this?

PHIL: What you watching *Crossroads* for?

GED: It helps me sleep.

(WATERS *taps the desk with a piece of chalk.*)

WATERS: If you've nearly finished . . .?

GED: Sorry, Mr. Waters.

PHIL (*suppressed mutter*): So you bloody should be . . .

CONNOR: How's the wife then, Ged?

GED (*simply*): All right.

WATERS: Bloody hell, what is this? We'll do sewing if you like . . . (*Some laughter.* GED *indicates his apology facially.*) Right, let's get you warm. (*Points to* MCBRAIN, *immediately to his right.*) Character. Stupid.

MCBRAIN (*fast, in character*): Excuse me, miss, where do I put this thing? (*Long pause.*) Oh . . .

WATERS (*to* SAMUELS, *next*): Ancient.

SAMUELS (*fast, in character*): Course I remember Moses. Little feller . . . (*Musing.*) . . . bad teeth, oy that breath . . .

WATERS (*to* CONNOR, *on end*): Sharp.

CONNOR: Erm . . . (*Furtive.*) Hey, wanna buy a spud?

WATERS: Sharp!

CONNOR (*wheedling*): A King Edward?

SAMUELS: Now you're talking.

> (WATERS *snorts, sustaining the speeded rhythms of the exercise.*)

WATERS (*to* PRICE, *end of left desk*): Feminine.

PRICE (*fast, perfect*): Four quid, dearie.

> (WATERS *thrown a little, perhaps by the unexpected harshness.*)

WATERS: Try another.

PRICE (*same voice*): . . . All I said was, all I *said was* . . . four quid doesn't cover sheets. . . . Just take your shoes off, is that a lot to ask?

WATERS (*to* GED MURRAY, *next*): Posh.

GED (*almost own voice, a strange modification, after thought*): Could you get me some clean bread for this dip, miss . . .?

WATERS: Nice. (*To* PHIL MURRAY.) Absent-minded.

PHIL (*bad Robb Wilton*): Al never forget——

CONNOR (*distinct whisper*): Whatsisname.

PHIL: Whatsisname. Look, piss off will you, Mick . . .?

WATERS: OK. Coming. It's speed . . . and it's detail. It's the detail inside the speed that makes the difference. A bit sluggish. We'll send it the other way. (*To* PHIL MURRAY.) Willy.

PHIL: Willy Nilly.

GED: Willy Won'ty.

PRICE: Willy Nocomebackagain.

CONNOR: Willy Ell.

SAMUELS (*pulling face*): God Villy . . .

MCBRAIN (*same face*): Willy Nands.

WATERS: God. (*To* MCBRAIN.) Sammy.

MCBRAIN: Sammy . . .?

WATERS: Yes, yes . . .

MCBRAIN (*desperate*): Sammy Circle.

WATERS (*urgent*): Right, come on.

SAMUELS (*very yiddish*): Sammyterwidyu?

CONNOR (*Italian*): 'Sa me you wanta see? Why dincha say so?

PRICE: Sammykazi. (*Pause.*) The Suicidal Shithouse.

GED (*singing*): Sammy, Sammy, you aren't half jammy . . .

PHIL: Sammy Professional.

MCBRAIN: Did someone call? I thought I heard my name.

16

WATERS: Not bad. Let's stretch it a bit. (*Stopwatch.*) Milk a cough. Go on, all of you.

MCBRAIN (*fluent*): By, she's coughing well tonight. What've you been doing to her, eh? Dirty thing, you.

SAMUELS: There's an old Indian remedy for coughing in women, you know. Full of spices and herbs and other Asian comestibles. Do you like that? Grub. It's a sort of curry linctus . . . (*Groans all round.*) They say it's very good . . .

PRICE (*perfectly acted*): Do you realize, we're all sharing the same air with that man. Just listen to him. (*Waits.*) Every time he does that there's a million infectious droplets joins the pool. He's emptying his lungs over everyone here. Go on, empty away, son, we don't mind . . .

CONNOR: I tell you what, why don't you come up here and cough and we'll all sit down there and laugh at you . . .

MCBRAIN: Mek a change for *your* act, Mick.

GED: I think she's trying to tell me something.

PHIL: Yeah, you're rubbish.

GED: Oh you speak the language do you? That's nice.

PHIL: Yes, I learnt it at school.

GED: Oh they dint teach us out like that. They taught us spittin'. And peein' up walls . . .

PHIL: Ay well, that's the secondary modern system for you intit. S'just a bad system.

MCBRAIN: I don't know whether she's coughing or having a baby. Nudge her and ask, would you, sir? She'll need oxygen whichever it is. Just . . . just coughing, I see, thank you, sir . . . there's room on that table over there, sir, if you, er. . . . Can't be too careful . . . I mean if those teeth aren't flush you could be in trouble.

SAMUELS: Bite you to death. Just imagine the headline in the *Evening News*: 'Man gnashed to death in clubland. Bronchitic woman's dentures held for questioning'.

MCBRAIN: Cough and the world coughs with you. Fart and you stand alone.

WATERS (*tough*): All right . . .

(PRICE *is already climbing up onto his desk.*)

PRICE: There was a young lady called Pratt . . .

MCBRAIN: Yes, yes . . .

PRICE: Who would hang from the light by her hat . . .

CONNOR: No, no.

PRICE: With a frightening cough . . .

SAMUELS: Yes.

PRICE: She would jerk herself off . . .

MCBRAIN: Ah . . .

PRICE (*vicious but quiet*): By sinking her teeth in her twat.

ALL: Olé!

(WATERS *stares at him. The others laugh, puzzled yet amused.*)

CARETAKER (*from doorway*): Smoking is not allowed on these
premises. Thank you. (*He turns again.*) Or standing on
desks. Or anything else like that.

(*He leaves with dignity.* PRICE *gets down, white, impassive,
avoiding* WATERS's *eyes, which follow him, close and tense as he
resumes his seat.*)

WATERS (*quiet, still*): Is somebody trying to tell me something?
(*Pause.*) Mmm? (*No answer.* PRICE *twangs a tiny violin
string, once, twice, three times. Slight sense of discomfiture as
they try to locate his meaning.*) The traitor distrusts truth.
(*They look at him.*) The traitor distrusts truth. Tongue
twisters. Shall we twist tongues, gentlemen?

(*They take it up in turn.*)

(*He calls.*) Faster.

(*The phrase gradually loses its shape and meaning in the
struggle for facility.* WATERS *sends it down* MCBRAIN's *line first,
then* PHIL MURRAY's, *so that we end on* PRICE.)

PRICE (*effortlessly, at speed*): The traitor distrusts truth. The
traitor distrusts truth. The traitor distrusts truth. The
traitor distrusts truth. The traitor distrusts truth. The
traitor distrusts truth. The traitor distrusts truth . . . (*Long
pause. Very levelly, measuredly, at* WATERS.) The traitor
distrusts truth.

WATERS (*finally, mild, matter-of-fact*): I've never liked the Irish,
you know. Dr. Johnson said they were a very truthful race,
they never spoke well of each other, but then how could
they have? (*They look around, faintly puzzled, amused.*) Big,
thick, stupid heads, large cabbage ears, hairy nostrils, daft

eyes, fat, flapping hands, stinking of soil and Guinness.
The niggers of Europe. Huge, uncontrollable wangers,
spawning their degenerate kind wherever they're allowed to
settle. I'd stop them settling here if I had my way. Send
'em back to the primordial bog they came from. Potato
heads.
(*Pause.* MCBRAIN *clenches and unclenches his fists on the desk,
watches them carefully.*)

CONNOR (*slowly*): Would that be Southern Irish or Northern
Irish, Mr. Waters?

WATERS (*mildly on*): Or Jews, for that matter.

SAMUELS: What you staring at me for?
(*Uneasy laughter, dying fast.*)

WATERS (*still very matter-of-fact*): They have this *greasy* quality,
do Jews. Stick to their own. Grafters. Fixers. Money.
Always money. Say Jew, say gold. Moneylenders, pawn-
brokers, usurers. They have the nose for it, you might
say. Hitler put it more bluntly: 'If we do not take steps to
maintain the purity of blood, the Jew will destroy civilization
by poisoning us all.' The effluent of history. Scarcely
human. Grubs.

SAMUELS (*unfunnily*): He must've met the wife's family.

WATERS: Negroes. Cripples. Defectives. The mad. Women.
(*Turning deliberately to* MURRAY'*s row.*) Workers. Dirty.
Unschooled. Shifty. Grabbing all they can get. Putting coal
in the bath. Chips with everything. Chips and beer. Trade
Unions dedicated to maximizing wages and minimizing
work. Strikes for the idle. Their greed. And their bottomless
stupidity. Like children, unfit to look after themselves.
Breeding like rabbits, sex-mad. And their mean vicious
womenfolk, driving them on. Animals, to be fed slops and
fastened up at night. (*Long pause.*) The traitor destroys the
truth.
(*Silence. Coughing. Shuffling of feet.*)

PRICE: Gone very dark in here all of a sudden.

MCBRAIN: Fancy a hand of crib?
(*Silence again.* WATERS *looks down at his desk. They exchange
inquiring looks across his space.*)

GED (*finally*): I don't get that. (*Pause.*) Were it some kind of a joke, Mr. Waters?

WATERS: Not exactly a joke, Mr. Murray.

GED: I mean. There's good and bad in everyone.

WATERS: Is there now?

CONNOR: Didn't you say so yourself?

WATERS: Did I?

SAMUELS: You're always saying it. 'A comic draws pictures of the world. The closer you look, the better you'll draw.' (*In the silence that follows, a penny begins to drop.*)

PRICE (*laconic, drawn out*): Lesson Three: 'Stereotypes'. (*Some faint embarrassment, the sense, however obscure, of having let* WATERS *down.*)

SAMUELS: You were having us on. That's a relief. I was beginning to get worried. (*Some relaxation, smiles, off the hook.*)

WATERS (*driving home*): If I've told you once I've told you a thousand times. We work *through* laughter, not *for* it. If all you're about is raising a laugh, OK, get on with it, good luck to you, but don't waste my time. There's plenty others as'll tek your money and do the necessary. Not Eddie Waters.

MCBRAIN (*conciliatory, apologetic*): So, a few crappy jokes, Mr. Waters . . .

WATERS: It's not the jokes. It's not the jokes. It's what lies behind 'em. It's the attitude. A real comedian—that's a daring man. He *dares* to see what his listeners shy away from, fear to express. And what he sees is a sort of truth, about people, about their situation, about what hurts or terrifies them, about what's hard, above all, about what they *want*. A joke releases the tension, says the unsayable, any joke pretty well. But a true joke, a comedian's joke, has to do more than release tension, it has to *liberate* the will and the desire, it has to *change the situation*. (*Pause.*) There's very little won't take a joke. But when a joke bases itself upon a distortion— (*At* PRICE, *deliberately.*)—a 'stereotype' perhaps—and gives the lie to the truth so as to win a laugh and stay in favour, we've moved away from a comic art and into the world of 'entertainment' and slick success. (*Pause.*) You're better than

20

that, damn you. And even if you're not, you should bloody well want to be.

CONNOR: I want to be famous. I want to be rich and famous. What's wrong with that, Mr. Waters?

WATERS: More than you want to be good?

MCBRAIN: What's wrong with being all three?

WATERS: Nothing. So long as you're good *first*. Because you'll never be good later.

PRICE (*suddenly*): Was it my limerick?

WATERS: I don't want to personalize this discussion . . .

PRICE: Oh, I see. You think talking to the six of us makes it impersonal, do you . . .?

PHIL: Oh, come on, Pricey, don't argue . . .

PRICE: Why not? He's accusing us . . . me . . . of doing some'at . . . immoral, I want to know what he means, it's pretty important to me . . .

SAMUELS: Look, we don't want a scene . . .

PRICE: Who wants a scene? I put a simple question. I'm just looking for a 'truth'. . . . Was it my limerick he took objection to? (*Pause.*) Because if it was, I'd like to know what his objections are, that's all.

SAMUELS: Well just don't push your luck, OK?

GED (*gentle but firm*): It's not up to you, Sammy.

WATERS: All right. Let's hear it again, Mr. Price.

PRICE: What?

WATERS: Will you recite it for us?

PRICE: What for?

WATERS: Give us a chance to look it over, see what we're dealing with.

PRICE: It was it then, was it?

WATERS: *You* think it was.

SAMUELS: Let's hear it then.

PHIL: Yeah, let's hear it.

(*Pause.* PRICE *bites his lip, sullen, moody.* WATERS *waits.*)

PRICE (*slowly*): All right.

> *There was a young lady called Pratt*
> *Who would hang from the light by her hat*
> *With a frightening cough*

> *She would jerk herself off*
> *By sinking her teeth in her twat.*
> (*Silence.*)

WATERS: It's clever. Is it your own?

PRICE: You could say that.

WATERS: How do you mean?

PRICE: I made it up. Just then.

WATERS: It's very clever.

GED (*marvelling*): You never made it up, did you?

PRICE: Look, Mr. Waters, I don't want compliments, just say what you don't like and we can get on . . .

WATERS: What do you think it says?

PRICE: I don't know. You tell me. I felt like saying it.

WATERS (*crossing to board, chalking up key words one beneath another; fast monotone*): Pratt. Pratt says twat. Lady, twat. Twat, bad word, unsayable. I've said it, will say it, might say it, *hat*, fooled you, build the suspense, cough, cough, jerked herself off, women masturbate, naughty, must say it now, dadadadadadada *twat. There!*

PRICE: So?

WATERS: It's a joke that hates women, Gethin.

PRICE: How come?

MCBRAIN: Ha ha. (*He shuts up quickly.*)

WATERS: It's a joke that hates women *and* sex. Do I go on?

PRICE (*cool*): Why not?

WATERS: In the Middle Ages men called the woman's sexual organ the devil's mark. According to Freud, men still see them as shark's mouths, in dreams. When you walk into that arena with a joke, you've gotta know why you're there.

PRICE: Maybe I'm just frightened.

WATERS: Maybe. But who do you blame, with your joke? Your lady 'jerks herself off'. Is she a man?

PRICE: It rhymes with cough.

WATERS: *Off* rhymes with cough. What do you *think* of your lady?

PRICE: Not a lot.

WATERS: Acrobatic but nasty? Sex-starved? Sex-mad? A nympho. Sexually insatiable.

22

MCBRAIN: Can I say something?

WATERS: By all means.

MCBRAIN: I mean, I do take your point and that, but doesn't his rhyme do just what you said you wanted? If fellers fear women and sex and that the way you say . . . doesn't that wee rhyme kind of . . . liberate the fear, sort of?

WATERS: I don't think it does. I think it recognizes it and *traps* it. Leaves it exactly where it is. Doesn't help it on. Doesn't do anything to *change* it. (*To everyone.*) Look, this is probably the last chance I'll get, and I want to state it as simply as I can. (*The door opens and an* ASIAN *enters, soaked and gleaming, small, slim, dark, delicate, a large muslin-wrapped something under his arm. He stops, smiles, shyly wavers. They turn to look at him. He leaves, closing the door behind him.* WATERS *crosses to the door after a moment, looks out down the corridor.*)

SAMUELS (*sotto voce*): If that's Challenor, we're all done for.

PHIL: Blacked up for the evening.

(WATERS *returns to his desk.*)

WATERS: A joke that feeds on ignorance starves its audience. We have the choice. We can say something or we can say nothing. Not everything true is funny, and not everything funny is true. Most comics *feed* prejudice and fear and blinkered vision, but the best ones, the best ones . . . illuminate them, make them clearer to see, easier to deal with. We've got to make people laugh till they cry. Cry. Till they find their pain and their beauty. Comedy is medicine. Not coloured sweeties to rot their teeth with.

(*The* ASIAN *reappears in the doorway.*)

Can I help you?

ASIAN: Please, Learning to Read?

WATERS: No . . .

ASIAN: Please. (*He puts down his parcel, fishes a leaflet from his sodden overcoat, hands it to* WATERS. WATERS *studies it, turns it over to read the other side.*) Learning to Read.

WATERS (*reading*): 'Reading to Learn'.

ASIAN: No. Learning to Read.

WATERS: No, it says Reading to Learn. (*He shows him.*) Reading. To. Learn. (*The* ASIAN *is perplexed.*) It says it's a class in

23

literary appreciation for intending students of the Open University. BBC. I'm no wiser than you, really . . .

ASIAN: A man gave it to me in the library . . .

WATERS: Aye, well he probably had a sense of humour.

ASIAN: Perhaps somewhere else . . .?

WATERS (*glancing at clock*): Look. I'll take you up to the Principal, he'll sort you out . . . (*He leads him towards door.*) I won't be a minute. Try and sort the order out while I'm away, will you, George. Look at you, you're soaked, man, how far've you come . . .?
(*They leave.*)

SAMUELS (*standing, lighting cigarette*): What a fuck up *this* is! (*At* PRICE.) Why don't you keep your bloody trap shut, eh?

MCBRAIN: Come on, Sammy.

SAMUELS: Fuck off. I want to think about me act, not arse the night away on . . . philosophy! Especially after he tells us we've got a bent adjudicator.

PHIL: Me too.

CONNOR: I thought you said you couldn't care less whether you did well or not tonight.

SAMUELS (*terse*): Well I do.

CONNOR: With having your own club and that up Moston way.

GED: Yeah. You said you could always employ yourself.

SAMUELS: Listen, cretin, do you wanna know something, I wouldn't be seen dead working a club like mine, I want the tops, I want TV, I want the Palladium. You can work my club, I'll book you as soon as you're ready, you're just what they need. As for that little git . . . (*Points at* PRICE, *turns away angrily.*)
(*Silence.*)

MCBRAIN: There was this poacher, see. And he shoots this deer. Big 'un. Hatstands in its head an' that. And he puts it over his back—like that—and he's hunking it off when this gamekeeper catches him and says, 'Hey, you're poaching', and your man says, 'How do you mean?' and he says, 'You've got a deer on your back', and he looks over his shoulder and he says, 'Get off.'
(*They laugh, more at the telling than the tale.* PRICE *gets up,*

24

steps onto the rostrum, becoming, in the movement, uncannily, the seventy-year-old WATERS.)

PRICE: Now, Mr. McBrain, you must see that that joke is totally supportive of all forms of blood sports. Besides which it undoubtedly hints at the dark secret of animal buggery or, at the very least, the stealthy buggering of men by beasts of the field and forest. A *comedian*, George, would have carried all this out into the open where we could all see it . . . (*He looks for it.*) . . . so that we'd all come to realize what should've been obvious from the start, or the Middle Ages, whichever you prefer: namely, deep down we all want fucking up the arse by antlered beasties. (*Pause.*) It's a joke that hates *deer*, George.

(MCBRAIN, CONNOR *and* PHIL MURRAY *laugh.* SAMUELS *scowls a bit in his corner.*)

GED (*serious*): That's not so funny.

PRICE (*sombre*): No. I suppose it isn't.

MCBRAIN: Why've you got it in for him then?

CONNOR: Yeah, what's that about? His favourite an' all. I thought you rated him.

PRICE: I don't want telling what to think. That's all. I don't want telling what to feel.

SAMUELS: You'd've felt my bleeding boot up your hole if you'd talked that way to me. Look at the fucking time . . .

PRICE (*quiet, with great, inquiring grace*): I didn't know you was Irish, Sammy . . .

(SAMUELS *laughs, a little slow splutter in spite of himself.*)

SAMUELS: You're a slippy fucker. Do you know that?

PRICE (*rolling eyes*): Yes, baas. I know that, baas. Yessuh baas. Whup ma hahd an cawl me kinky.

MCBRAIN: Answer the question. Why're you so bent on riling the old man? *He's* no different.

PRICE: So maybe I am. (*He strokes his cropped head, an unconscious gesture.*)

CONNOR: Yeah. Maybe it's more than your hairs you've been losing. (PRICE *turns away, smiling.*) I'll tell you some'at. He's a good old man. And he's a comic to his toenails. He doesn't *need* to do this for peanuts, you know, every

Friday night, *here*, on two quid an hour or whatever it is. He could take a room in a pub and charge a fortune and he'd get it too. So that he can teach pricks like us he does it. (*Pause.*) And if I get out of the building game and earn a living doing what I want to do more than anything else, always have done, I'll have him to thank and no one else. (*Deliberately.*) And that goes for everyone here, whether they know it or not.

GED: It goes for me.

MCBRAIN: Yeah.

PHIL: All right, he's a genius, what is this, Gala Night at the City Varieties?

GED: *We* knew less than nowt.

PHIL: Speak for yourself. I'd done clubs . . .

GED: Two. Ardwick and Oldham. One of 'em withheld your money. The other called you a taxi to drive you off to safety.

PHIL: Like the bloody wild west, both of 'em. There was nothing wrong with *me*. My troubles started when I took you on, believe me.

GED (*quiet, toughly serious*): When are you gonna face it: you're not funny. You're a straight. You can't work on your own. (*Pause.*) But I can.

PHIL: Try it.

GED: Maybe I will.

MCBRAIN: Frying tonight, by God! Jees, listen to 'em go. All of 'em. Those poor bloody guinea pigs of an audience at this club'll know the meaning of tears tonight, by Christ, won't they just. Come on, let's get the order decided, who wants to go first? Sammy? How about you?

SAMUELS: No thanks.

MCBRAIN: Anyone? (*Nobody.*) OK. (*Takes pack of cards from his pocket, cuts it twice.*) Lowest loses, aces high. (*He deals five cards in sequence to correspond to the five turns. They peer at the cards.*)

CONNOR: Shit!

MCBRAIN: You Mick? Tough.

CONNOR: Ah well. At least they'll be awake.

SAMUELS: You'll no doubt manage to do something about it though . . .

MCBRAIN: Second, Sammy?

SAMUELS: All right.

MCBRAIN: Ged? Phil?

GED: OK.

MCBRAIN (*looking at* PRICE): How do you feel about last?

PRICE: All the same to me.

MCBRAIN: Right. Top of the bill, kidda. Will they be waiting for you! Now, who wants music? (*They show,* MCBRAIN *writes it down.*) Gethin, you have music don't you?

PRICE: No.

MCBRAIN: I thought you got off with that song. What was it . . .?

PRICE: No, I've changed it. No music.

SAMUELS: You're a cool sod, I'll give you that. The bleeding nerve of it, working up an act for three months and then altering it half an hour before he goes on. You'll come a right cropper one day, you will. I can feel it in me water.

PRICE (*deliberately*): Well, piss over somebody else for a change, Sammy.

MCBRAIN: Hey, hey, hey, any more of that and you'll go in the book . . . (*He brandishes a book in his right hand, a referee.*) (WATERS *in, followed by the* ASIAN. WATERS *carries a tray with eight teas in plastic cups, spoons, sugar.*)

WATERS: I got the teas in. (*They move towards the tray.*) Gentlemen, this is Mr. Patel.

GED: Hello, Mr. Patel.

(*A few more grunts of acknowledgement.*)

MCBRAIN: Hey, if you've got any good jokes, I'll have a word with you before you go . . .

(PATEL *smiles innocently.*)

WATERS: Mr. Patel is going to stay with us for a little while, I've promised him a lift into town on the way down to the Club. He's, erm . . . he's been sent on a wild goose chase . . . and the monsoon is still with us, as you'll no doubt have observed for yourselves. Sit there if you would, Mr. Patel, by the pipes. Take your coat off if you like.

27

PATEL (*sitting*): Thank you no, sir. I'm very comfortable, please . . .

(WATERS *resumes the desk, picks up* MCBRAIN's *list*.)

MCBRAIN: That's the order.

WATERS: Fine. And the asterisks are music, yes?

MCBRAIN: Ahunh.

WATERS (*at clock*): Right. I don't want anything from your acts from now on, all right. Just let them lie and get yourselves limber. OK. Close your eyes. Come on, close your eyes. (*They close their eyes, frowning or amused.*) Now think. Think about yourselves. What you've been, what you've done, what you are, what you want. All right? Keep thinking. Now, take one incident, anything, any little thing, that means something to you, maybe something that embarrasses you or haunts you or still makes you frightened, something you still can't deal with maybe, all right? Now think about it. It may be some'at very gentle, very tender, some'at you said, some'at you did, wanted to do. . . . All right. Open up. (*They blink at each other.*)

GED: Bloody hellfire, I were just gettin' into that.

WATERS: Let's hear it then, Mr. Murray.

GED (*and others*): What?

WATERS: I want you to tell it. Any way you like, in your own time. (*Pause.*) But make it funny.

GED: Jesus wept!

SAMUELS: He'd been watching your act.

GED: I were thinking about wife.

MCBRAIN: Haha. Very good, very good. It's the way he tells 'em you know.

WATERS (*softly*): You're next, George. (*To* GED.) So tell us about it. Be funny. Try.

GED: She went in hospital, have the nipper. Ancoats. Bout two in the morning. He musta lay there best part of a year, all snug like, planning it. I rang up from Beswick depot next morning about half-five. Nothing. Seven, nothing. Half-nine. Half-ten. I musta bin nervous, I found mesel smoking me own fags. I went to our mother's dinnertime, for company I suppose. (*Difficult now.*) Me dad'd been off

28

work for a while, Clayton Aniline . . . he'd had a sorta
breakdown . . . (*He touches his head.*) . . . gone a bit queer in
the head . . .

PHIL: Bloody hell, what you talkin' about that for . . .?

GED: Anyroad, I rang again and they said she'd had it so I got
a bus and went down. (*Pause.*) When I got to the ward, I
couldn't go in.

CONNOR: The door was locked.

GED: I suddenly thought, what if it runs in the family.

MCBRAIN: Like crabs, you mean.

GED: I thought, what if there's some'at wrong with it. (*Silence
now, the story rivets.*) She were holding it in her arm. I saw
it ten beds away. Black hair. Red face. Little fists banging
away on wife's face. (*Pause.*) He were bloody perfect. He
were bloody perfect.
(*He looks around, unembarrassed, largely unaware of his
effect. Some coughs, stirrings, sniffs.*)

PHIL (*mutter*): What you talkin' about that for?

GED (*simply*): I were thinkin' about it.

PHIL: You were thinking about it. Jesus wept.

MCBRAIN: I'm not following that, Mr. Waters. No thanks.

PRICE: I went nutty once.

SAMUELS (*queer*): Well, you do surprise me, Gethin.

WATERS: Is that what you were thinking about?

PRICE: Sort of.

WATERS: Go on.

PRICE: I thumped a teacher.

CONNOR: Oh the hard bastard of a thing you are.

PRICE (*simply*): Not really. Were a woman. She called us a
guttersnipe. In music. I clocked her one. It seemed the
only thing I could do. She went white. Whiter than me even.
Then she cried. Little tears. They sent me to a psychologist.
Thirteen. Me I mean, *he* were a bit older. Though not much.
We developed a sort of tolerant hatred of each other. He
kept insisting on treating me as an equal, you know.
Patronizing me. The last time I saw him he gave me this
long piece and he said, 'You see, Gethin, basically all any of
us want is to be loved.' And I said, 'If you know so much,

29

how come you wear a Crown Topper?' (*Pause.*) That's when
I decided I'd be a comedian.
(*He sniffs, twangs the violin string.*)

GED: That's about as funny as mine.

PHIL: Yeah, laugh a minute.

WATERS: It's hard isn't it. Not exactly queuing up to go, are we,
gentlemen? (*He scans* MCBRAIN's *row, then stares at* PHIL
MURRAY.) Why *is* that, do you think? It wouldn't have been
all waste, Mr. Murray, if your child had been born defective,
would it? I mean, it would at least have afforded us a worthy
subject for the comic's wit. (*Pause.*) Do we fear . . . other
people . . . so much that we must mark *their* pain with
laughter, our own with tears? People deserve respect because
they are people, not because they are known to us. Hate
your audience and you'll end up hating yourself. All right.
We'll stop that there . . . (*Looks at clock: about 8.20.*) Any
final queries about your spots? George? Sammy? (*Both give
negatives.*) Mick?

CONNOR (*fiddling*):Y'aven't a dickie have you, this keeps fallin'
off . . .?

WATERS: I'll have a look at it in the van going down. Gethin?
(PRICE *shakes his head.*) Sure? (PRICE *nods.*) What about you
two?

PHIL: We're fine, Mr. Waters.

WATERS (*to everyone*): I want to wish you luck. You worked
hard, you've sweated, you've been honester than most.
I'll be pulling for you all tonight. And you'll *know* if you're
good. You'll not need tellin'.
(CHALLENOR *knocks, enters on the knock. He's maybe five
years younger than* WATERS, *rather waxen, discreetly dressed,
with a homburg, and umbrella, which he shakes. His self-regard
is almost a mannerism, though he retains a residual lithe
charm.*)

CHALLENOR: Evening, Eddie. I'll never understand why they
don't run boats to Manchester.

WATERS: We're waiting on London to give the word. Hello,
Bert.

CHALLENOR: Spry as ever. Eddie Waters, the Lancashire Lad.

WATERS: Relax. You'll see forty, don't you fret.

CHALLENOR: I thought you'd have taken the bungalow at Southport by now, Eddie.

WATERS: Nay. I'm a Manchester man. I'd miss the rain. (*The relaxed yet glinting spat ends.*)

CHALLENOR: These your lads, then?

WATERS: Aye. Mr. Challenor of the C.A.M.F., Phil and Ged Murray, Gethin Price, Mick Connor, Sammy Samuels, George McBrain.

CHALLENOR: How do you do. (*He's looking in* PATEL's *direction, inquiringly.*)

WATERS: He's not part of the class.

CHALLENOR: No? There's one or two about, you know. Midland clubs. Awful lot of people, of course . . .

WATERS: Is there anything you want to say before we get down there?

CHALLENOR (*checking watch*): I wouldn't mind a word or two, Eddie. Is it far?

WATERS: No. No. Ten minutes. (*The* CARETAKER *comes in. He carries a shattered lectern.*)

CARETAKER (*to* WATERS): I told the Principal you were looking for him. (*He points in* PATEL's *direction.*) He's back now. He had to go down to the other centre in Beswick. (*He makes a drinking sign with his right hand.*)

WATERS: Thank you, I think we can manage now . . .

CARETAKER: I told him you were looking. He's in his office. Waiting.

WATERS: It's very good of you.

CARETAKER (*looking at lectern*): They've gone bloody *mad* down there, that Karate lot. (*He leaves.*) (CHALLENOR *looks at* WATERS.)

CHALLENOR: Don't mind me, Eddie. (WATERS *doesn't want to leave, can't show it.*)

WATERS: We'll go and see the Principal, Mr. Patel, just to make sure you're in the wrong place. (PATEL *crosses behind him to the door. To class.*) I'll be back . . . (*They leave.* CHALLENOR *mounts the dais carefully, stands at the tall, sloping desk, places his black attaché case on the ledge.*)

CHALLENOR: Going to give me a good show then?

MCBRAIN: That we are. Crème de la crème. You'll laugh tonight, Mr. Challenor, that you will.

CHALLENOR: That's good news, brother. It's been a particularly unfunny day.

SAMUELS: Your worries are over, Mr. Challenor, mark my words. Five of the finest comedy acts west of Royton. I'm *very* funny.

CHALLENOR: I'll watch out for you.

SAMUELS: Trap three. It'll guide in.

PHIL: I saw you at the Hulme Hippodrome just after the war, about 1951. Frank Randle top of the bill. Bert Challenor, the Cockney Character.

CHALLENOR: Right. Played Number Ones for twenty years, right through to the end. History to you lot . . .

PRICE: Did you really play with Frank Randle?

CHALLENOR: I did.

PRICE: What were he like? Were he one of the best?

CHALLENOR: Best of his kind, I suppose.

PRICE: How do you mean, of his kind?

CHALLENOR: He was *local*, wasn't he? South of Birmingham he was nothing. A whole set of 'em—Sandy Powell, Albert Modley, Jimmy James. George was the giant. Took the country. George was the great one. He's the one to study, if you're keen to get on.

PRICE: Formby?

CHALLENOR: Ahunh.

CONNOR: Didn't Mr. Waters work with your man before the war?

CHALLENOR: Eddie did a lot of things before the war.

SAMUELS: Was he good?

(*Pause.*)

CHALLENOR: He were brilliant.

SAMUELS: Yeah? What happened then?

CHALLENOR (*quietly*): He didn't . . . want enough. (*Pause.*) I don't know. He just stayed up here . . .

(*Pause.*)

PRICE: Have you seen Randle's films? I've seen 'em all. He's untouchable. (*He gets up suddenly, assumes an uncanny Frank*

32

Randle stance and gait.) 'I'm as full of vim as a butcher's dog—I'm as lively as a cricket. Baaa, I'll sup it if it keeps me up all neet. I'll take anybody on of my age and weight, dead or alive, and I'll run 'em, walk 'em, jump 'em, fight 'em, aye, and I'll play 'em dominoes. Baaa, I've supped some stuff toneet. Listen, ony t'other day I went to a funeral, I were stood at graveside, a chap looked at me, he said, How old are yer? I said eighty-two, he said I'm eighty-four. I said, I don't think it's much use thee going home at all.'

(*The group laugh.* CHALLENOR *smiles thinly, undazzled.*)

CHALLENOR: Try it in Bermondsey, sonny. Try it in Birmingham even.

PHIL: Pay him no heed, Mr. Challenor.

SAMUELS: He argues like other people breathe.

CHALLENOR: Well. Nice meeting you. Good luck for tonight.
(*He dwells, enjoying the attention.*) A couple of . . . hints. Don't try to be deep. Keep it simple. I'm not looking for philosophers, I'm looking for comics. I'm looking for someone who sees what the people want and knows how to give it them. It's the people pay the bills, remember, yours, mine . . . Mr. Waters's. We're servants, that's all. They demand, we supply. Any good comedian can lead an audience by the nose. But only in the direction they're going. And that direction is, quite simply . . . escape. We're not missionaries, we're suppliers of laughter. I'd like you to remember that. See you down there. Oh. A text for tonight. Perhaps we can't all be Max Bygraves. But we can try.
(*He takes his leave. Silence.* MCBRAIN *opens another two cans of 'E', hands one to* CONNOR. SAMUELS *lights a panatella. They sit looking at each other, scanning for concern or alarm.*)

SAMUELS (*disgust staining his voice*): Oh, that's marvellous. That's . . . marvellous.

PHIL (*backing his chair to the floor savagely as he stands*): What the fuck are we gonna do?

SAMUELS: We're gonna get the bum's rush, that's what we're gonna do.

33

MCBRAIN: Not at all. What're you on about?

SAMUELS: Look, you heard him, Seamus . . .

MCBRAIN (*thinking, already doubtful*): He had to say that. He's an old enemy of the Boss's, what else could he say?

PHIL: Sod that, what're we gonna *do*?

GED: What's that supposed to mean? We're gonna do our act.

PHIL: He'll murder us. You've got to be joking.

MCBRAIN: That's very nearly funny.

GED (*to* PHIL, *standing heavily*): Look, what are you talking about?

PRICE (*piercing through the din*): He means—do you not?—how can you change your act at this short notice to suit Challenor. Isn't that what you mean? (*He takes in the whole group in the silence that follows the question. People sniff, shuffle, look at others.*)

SAMUELS (*finally*): It's not such a tragedy. I can paste some'at together. Fortunately, I've managed to keep my distance . . .

CONNOR: Challenor'll get the act I came with. He don't bother me.

SAMUELS: OK, so be the funniest hod-carrier at Wimpey's.

CONNOR (*steely*): I don't carry a hod, Sammy.

GED: We've got an act . . .

PHIL: We've got several acts. What about the one we used Christmas?

GED: What? You heard what Mr. Waters thought of that . . .

PHIL: Look, Ged, I mean, look, fuck Mr. Waters, I don't intend to spend the rest of my days on the pigging knocker collecting club money. Now I don't. All right?

GED (*implacable*): I don't care what you do or don't do tomorrow. Tonight, we do the act.

PHIL: Do we.

GED: We do.

PHIL: You're stupid.

GED (*dangerous, very swift*): No, Phil. Leave it.
(PRICE *watches them all from a distance, limbering up.*)

SAMUELS: What about you, George?

MCBRAIN: I'll think of something. Well known you know for my flexibility. In any case (*Frank Carson voice*) it's the way

34

that I tell 'em . . .

PHIL (*splenetic*): If you hate those bloody docks as much as you claim, you'll know what to do all right.

SAMUELS: Somebody shoulda told Challenor they *do* run boats to Manchester. So that pricks like you can unload 'em.

MCBRAIN (*simply*): I know what to do. Trust Georgey.

(*Pause.* SAMUELS *turns to* PRICE.)

SAMUELS: Whorrabout you then?

(PRICE *is doing left-leg squats on the dais. Stops carefully. Swivels gracefully round.*)

PRICE (*innocent*): Me?

SAMUELS: *You*, you slippy sod.

PRICE (*distinctly*): The traitor distrusts truth. The traitor distorts truth. The traitor destroys truth.

SAMUELS: You're dafter than you think, you know.

PRICE (*inward*): I drive a van all day for British Rail. And if Challenor were on fire I wouldn't piss him out. Max Bygraves! (*The venom muscles his throat.*)

MCBRAIN (*quietly*): Maybe you won't have to? (PRICE'*s raised eyebrows ask the question.*) You've changed your act already, haven't you. Who's a clever boy then?

SAMUELS (*sourly marvelling*): Slippy.

(*Silence.* GED *frowns concern.* CONNOR *watches.* MCBRAIN *chuckles.* SAMUELS *clicks his teeth.* PHIL MURRAY *flops back in his chair.* PRICE *stands a moment longer, then moves for his gear, gathers it, turns, begins to leave.*)

PRICE: See you at the show, darlings . . .

(*He's gone, out on amazing tiptoe, like a dancer in a minefield.*)

SAMUELS (*following slowly to door*): Waters musta mentioned Challenor, told him last week, after the lesson. They allus have a drink together in the Mare . . .

CONNOR (*far from content*): Forget it, for Christ's sake. Who cares about bloody Challenor . . .

(*He gathers his things roughly, angrily: leaves. The others begin to gather their belongings.* WATERS *back in. He carries six buttonholes in plastic bags. Looks at depleted company.*)

WATERS: Ah, the others have gone on, have they. . . . I brought one of these each for you. . . . Here . . . (*He hands four out,*

35

pockets the remainder.) Don't start boozing after your turn. I've promised the Principal we'll be out by ten at the latest. All set then? Let's get the van . . .

(*They troop out one after the other,* WATERS *standing in the doorway to see them through.*

He gives a final cursory look around the room and leaves, closing door behind him.

Sounds of footsteps, muffled talking. After a moment, car and van doors being opened and closed, engines starting up.

The door opens and the CARETAKER *peeps in, sees the room vacated, advances. He carries a smashed chair, the frame in the right hand, a leg in the left.*

After a moment he sights PATEL's *muslin-covered package. Stops, scans. Signs of slight but rising apprehension. He reaches gingerly towards it with the chair leg. Touches. Prods more vigorously, yet still cringing from it, as though half-expecting an explosion. Nothing. He drops the chair leg, opens the neck of the bag, peers in, sniffs, sniffs again, sniffs several times, his face crinkling with disgust. Stands. Picks up his chair. Leaves, switching off all lights behind him.*)

ACT TWO

A small club stage, lit but empty save for a microphone. In front of it, on opposite sides, WATERS *and* CHALLENOR *sit with their drinks at red formica-top tables. Club pianist, small, bored, at piano on stage, behind the acts. Relaxed chatter and clink, in this lull. A buzzer sounds, calling silence. The concert* SECRETARY *(unseen) makes the announcement over the loudspeaker. (Perhaps the concert* SECRETARY *is seen.)*

SECRETARY (*off*): Yes, yes, all right, Teddie. I'll see to it after the draw . . . (*This to someone off mic.*) And now, ladies and gentlemen, your kind attention, please . . . (*The noise barely alters.*) I'm waiting for your kind attention, ladies and gentlemen . . . I don't want to wait all night. Thank you. . . . (*Quiet.*) . . . As announced in last week's club bulletin, there will now be a brief interval in the bingo . . . (*Groans, calls of 'No'.*) . . . it's been announced, it's been announced . . . *a brief* interval in the bingo to listen to some new comics setting their feet on the first rung of the ladder of fame. Now this'll last half an hour at the most and I'd like you to show these lads the traditional courtesy of the club and then we'll get straight back to bingo as soon as it's over. Now these are all lads who've been coached by that favourite comic of yesteryear, the Lancashire Lad himself, Mr. Eddie Waters. Take a bow, Eddie, that's it. (WATERS *bows from the piano: some applause.*) So I think we're in for a treat. . . . First off then, a young man from Ireland, now domiciled in Moss Side, your welcome please for . . . Mick . . . Connor.
(CONNOR *appears from the wings, in hired evening dress and black pumps, a white carnation and black dickie.*)

CONNOR (*very Irish*): I told him not to say anythin' about me bein'

Irish. I wanted to creep up on yez like, you know. Good
evening. Sorry about de bingo. Wuz yez ever foreigners,
anny of yer? I don't mean the odd fortnight at Southport, I
mean like always? Jeez, it's a funny thing. First day in
Manchester I go in this public house, I orders a pint of dark,
this man says to me, been in two minutes, Why don't you go
home where you come from? Get back to Moss Side. True.
That was before the blacks come to help us out, shoulder
some of the white man's burden. I went off fer digs. Your
woman opens the door, a neat little thing wi' gouty eyes,
she said (*Huge voice.*) No Irish, no Scots, no Welsh, no
West Indians, no Pakistanis, no Chinese, no Lapps. I said:
How come you left out Eskimos? She said: I never *had*
Eskimos, and closed the door. Troublemakers, I never
knew we wuz troublemakers till I got to England. You don't,
you know. I mean, what are you lot, eh, do you know?
You don't find out, do you? Just people. You'd have to go
to India or . . . Africa . . . or Ireland to find out. Mmmm??
They'd tell yer right enough. Well, stick around, maybe
they'll come to you. You know, even the Catholic Church is
different here. I went to Mass at the Holy Name, like a
bloody opera. Back home in Wexford it's more like a market.
The priest charges ten per cent commission on all
transactions. And confessions . . . Jesus . . . here you can
hear the candles melt, so you can . . . your Irish priest is
either half-deaf or half-cut, so you've gotta burst your lungs
off to get absolution, safact. (*Bellows.*) Bless me, Father, for
I have sinned, it is six years since my last confession . . .
(*Own voice.*) *Then* you can hear a pin drop . . . (*Priest's voice,
drunk.*) Speak up, my son, there's nothing to be ashamed of
now, the Lord welcomes sinners, big and small . . . (*Bellows.*)
I have missed Mass seven hundred and twenty-three times . . .
I have fornicated. (*Own voice.*) No snobs in Wexford. No
holier than thous. I tell yer, we'd sit there by the box every
Saturday night . . . picking up girls for the ceilidh . . . all
the young buckos . . . (*Acting it.*) Hey, dissun's a goer . . .
ten times widat Heaney feller from Clanmancoise. . . . Hey,
wait while you hear where he put his finger . . . (*He laughs.*)

None of that here mind. Yer English priest enjoys it too much. . . . Oh yes. (*English priest's voice, dripping with retracted interest, low and breathy, close to mic.*) Yes, I see, my son, and *you* put your hand where? (*Self, very low, hesitant but intense.*) I put it . . . down her mouth, father. (*Priest, slight but controlled increase in excitement.*) Did you now? Erm . . . and why did you do that, my son? (*Self.*) She 'ad dis . . . bone stuck, father . . . (*Own voice.*) Or there's the other sort, the feller that's gonna end up Bishop's secretary, he's very bored . . . (*Bored posh priest, testy.*) All right, so you've been wearing your sister's clothes again, don't you ever do anything else . . .? Don't you fancy your mother's . . .? I mean, you're in here every week with the same story, there's no development, there's no plot, look, it might excite you, there's absolutely nothing in it for me. Your penance is five Our Fathers and five Hail Marys and the next time you're tempted to get into a frock just . . . count to ten, all right . . . and ask God to make you a little more inventive. (*Yawn.*) Next. (*Pause.*) Reminds me of the old spinster lady back home—confesses fornication and the priest asks her for details while he gets a good sight of her through the grill, so she tells him about this wonderful night of love she spent with a tinker, and the priest says, Mary McGuire, that's a most shameful thing you did and you a respected spinster of seventy-three. And she says, as a matter of fact I was thirty when it happened, I just like talking about it. (*Pause.*) I married an English Catholic girl you know. On the pill she was. (*Dialogue.*) How come you're on the pill? (*Her.*) Our church says we must search our own individual consciences for the truth and then act accordingly. (*Self.*) Did y'ever hear such a thing? Dem's what we call *Protestants* in Ireland. So she's sitting on the bed on the honeymoon, I see her take these little yaller things out, I says what's that, she says the pill, why, can't you take it in Ireland, and I says, Oh, I can take it, it's the women is barred. Actually, the Cardinal did say Irish women could take the pill and the Holy Church herself gave instructions on how they were to be administered. Only, as soon as the woman'd get up next morning, the bloody thing'd fall out. Course we had other ways. An uncle of mine practised coitus interruptus all his life. God . . . (*Long reflective pause.*) *He* was a sad man, though. So listen anyway. Don't believe all you hear, you know what I mean. Speak well of the living. Especially within earshot. Next time you meet an Irishman, count to ten . . . and ask God to make you more inventive. And don't keep slapping him on the back. One day he'll stick a pack of dynamite up his jacket and blow your bloody arm off. If he didn't do it already. (*He turns round, there's a huge charged gap in his coat and shirt.*) Good-night, God bless.

(*Pianist plays through* CONNOR's *applause and exit.*)

SECRETARY (*mic.*): A Manchester man now, from Middleton, a warm welcome please for . . . (*Reading.*) Mr. Sammy Samuels.

(SAMMY *walks on, trailing a hand-mic. He wears a fine fitting white jacket, red carnation, black bow, black handkerchief, diamond cufflinks.*)

SAMUELS: A black Irish Jew, with a limp, and a stammer, half-blind, and eczema, and leaking sores up his nose, and this club foot, with woodworm and piles (*He does all this, very minimally but well.*) was looking for digs. That was four years ago, I wonder what happened to him. Nice place you've got here, where'd you hang the Bronco? Have you always come here? (*Peering down at the tables.*) Did you come tonight? Evening, sir. Nice out? I might get mine out in a minute. Sit down, lady, we'll have no rushing the stage, I don't care how attractive you find me. Look at that. (*He barrels his chest, flexes a bicep, turns for a latissimus dorsi, ends up pointing gently at his profiled nose.*) Not an ounce of fat, I defy you to find one, nineteen-twenty-nine I were born. Year of the Great Crash. The sound of me father's jaw droppin'. He took one look at me and divorced the old lady. He wasn't even Jewish. Abraham Isaac Immanuel Moishe Jankowitz ben Tattersall. Had a stand on Tib Street market. Selling beads to Africans. Did well. So, in the divorce court, the judge delivers his judgement on the alimony. He says this court grants the wife eighty pounds a month maintenance.

And the old man says: Judge, dat's very generous of you
and to tell you de truth ven business gets better I'll maybe
also help out a little. The old woman brought us all up on
her own. Well, more or less, she found a few long-lost
uncles from Didsbury now and then. Me sister went to
university. She comes back after the first term and says I'm
afraid I can't continue with my studies, Momma. Vy? she
says. She couldn't say why. Vy. Always vy. Vy? she says.
Well, I don't know how to put it, Momma, I'm, er, sorta
pregnant. Vot? You're pregnant? Do you know how I've
struggled giving you de education I never got, now you
come back you say you pregnant? Give me a chair, give me
a seltzer. Oi, oi. She sits down. So who's de fadder? Like
that. So who's de fadder? My sister says I'm not sure, it's
difficult to say, Momma, I can't . . . pinpoint the father. . . .
You don't know de fadder? Vot you saying! I send you to
university. I'm simple people, I'm plain but you're educated,
I don't know de proper vay to be introduced, but you don't
know how to ask 'Mit who am I having de pleasure?' The
bank manager rang her. Mrs. Samuels, I've gotta tell you
you're overdrawn fifty pounds. Is dat so? she says. So vot
vos de balance two months ago? He looks, he says: You had
credit of sixty-four pounds. OK, she says, and did I phone
you? (*He reaches the cobbled area of the turn here. Improvises
clumsily.*) You're very fortunate here . . . ladies and
gentlemen . . . because tonight . . . I'm about to reveal to
you . . . things about myself as've never bin revealed before.
Anywhere. (*Saucy stare.*) I married well. Beautiful, gifted,
young, educated, rich. Honeymoon in Majorca. Great
Birmingham as it's known over there. I lay on the bed
smoking a cigar while she gets undressed and she says I'd
like you to know I've slept with half the men in West
Didsbury. And I poured myself another glass of champagne,
puffed on the cigar, sucked a date and smiled. I mean, how
big's West Didsbury? A man orders lobsters in a restaurant,
a hip black waiter serves him. Vaiter, I esk for lobster, how
come you bring me a lobster vid only von claw? The black
guy smiles, stoned out of his head. So maybe it was in a

fight, man, he says. So maybe you bring me the vinner? says
Abie. I've nothing against blacks, you understand. I mean,
they're the only thing keeping you from me, let's face it. I
saw a West Indian lying down in Market Street about five
o'clock in the afternoon, traffic whirling all around him. A
feller went up to him and said: What you doing there?
and the West Indian says: I just fell out of a fourth-floor
window of Woolworth's, and the white feller looks at him and
feels his biceps and he says: If you don't mind me asking,
how much did they want for you? Did you read about 'em
burning them Pakistanis' houses down? They burnt one house,
the man had two wooden legs, he was burnt to the ground,
poor sod. Do you like Irish jokes? Flanagan and Monaghan
working a trench. Flanagan brings Monaghan a massive
thump on the side of the head with his sledgehammer.
Monaghan calls out, For God's sake be careful, Flanagan,
you're after making me bite my lip. I'm afraid, Mrs.
Monaghan, your husband will never work again. She says:
I'll go in and tell him, it might cheer the poor man up a bit.
Irish farmer and his lad, both lazy buggers, sprawled there
in the kitchen and the father says, Patrick, go out and see if
it's raining, and Patrick says, Ah sure, can you not call in the
dog and see if he's wet? Smart, see. They published a book:
'The Wit and Wisdom of the Irish: Twenty Years of Social
Security'. What do you think of Women's Lib then? Burnt
your bras, have you? (*Sniffs.*) Some'at's burning. I burnt the
wife's. She played hell, she was still in it. We had the house
surrounded by neighbours screaming, Put out that pig, you'll
have the Rabbi round. No. I think women get a raw deal. I
mean it's nothing but decisions decisions for 'em, is it? Shall
I get up at ten or eleven? Who shall I spread the word about
today? Whose house can I be at when he gets home . . .?
There's no end to it. This Women's Lib woman collared me
in a bar, she says: You're a brutal, loudmouthed, irrational,
sadistic, sexist, male, chauvinist pig, you're nothing else. I
said: (*Low, wheedling voice.*) There's no chance of a quick
shag is there? Can't get enough of it. I had the managing
director's wife, firm I used to work for. I got this letter from

42

him: My dear sir, I am fully aware of your relations with my wife. Be at my office at eleven sharp Monday. I wrote back: Dear sir, your circular letter received. Will attend conference on time. One more. A converted prostitute, beating the drum in the Sally Army, crowd round her. Yes, I once lay in the arms of men. Boom, she goes, I sinned. Boom, I smoked. Boom. I drank gin. Boom. Boom. Night after night I gambled away my youth and happiness. Look at me now—changed—Boom—converted—Boom—washed in the blood of the Lamb. What do I do on a Saturday night now? I stand on street corners beating this bleeding drum! Boom, boom. Good-night and God bless. (*Nods at pianist, breaks into 'When You're Smiling'. Ends.*) (*He takes his bows and applause. Looks defiantly once in* WATERS's *direction, leaves stage.*)

SECRETARY (*mic.*): Two lads now from Blackley, a double act, Phil and Ged Murray, who call themselves . . . Night and Day.

(*A large trunk wheeled on, followed by* PHIL MURRAY. PHIL *carries a small girl dummy, shy, long blonde hair.*)

PHIL (*a good 'best' voice*): Good evening, ladies and gentlemen. Say good evening, Sophie.

DOLL (*eyelashes demure*): Good evening.

PHIL: Are you ready to sing your song then, Sophie?

GED (*strangulated, from box: minimal but effective dummy voice*): Hey.

PHIL (*ignoring him*): What's it going to be then, Sophie?

GED (*louder*): Hey. I'm talking to you.

PHIL (*side of mouth*): Shut up. Sophie?

GED: Listen. I'm not lying here all bloody night. Have you got that stupid stick-doll in 'ere?

PHIL: Be quiet.

GED: Y'ave, 'aven't you? Y'ave. You mighta lain 'im down.

PHIL: Excuse me, Sophie . . . (*He opens the trunk, places the* DOLL *on* GED's *stomach, closes it again.*) Ladies and gentlemen, we *were* going to start with a song . . .

GED (*to the* DOLL *in the trunk*): Hey, stop that, stop it, *stop* it! (*To* PHIL.) Look, I've told you about this one, get 'er off me, come on . . .

(PHIL *begins to get* GED *out from the trunk. It's a painful floppy process. They flounder to the tall stool by the mic. Their patter throughout is serious, desperate.*)

PHIL (*fixing him on his thigh*): Right, now sit there and sit still. (GED'S *dressed in Manchester City supporters' colours, scarf, woollen hat, rattle, rosette. A fair vent's dummy. He slips off, is dragged back, all in one movement. Perches finally.*)

GED: I've told you before about that stick-doll . . .

PHIL: Shut up.

GED: I've got splinters all over my——

PHIL: Never mind the splinters.

GED: Keep your legs still. What you doing, reliving a knee-trembler?

PHIL: That's enough. (GED *grins at the Audience.*)

GED (*from side of mouth*): Face front and keep smiling. *Smile,* you fool. They might go away.

PHIL: Where have you been then?

GED (*scanning Audience*): They're canvas. Somebody's been painting 'em during the break. What?

PHIL: I said where have you been?

GED (*deliberately posh*): Where have I *been*? I've *been* to me father's cremation haven't I? (*Waves rattle, own voice.*) He were a City fan. (*Rattle.*) Colin Bell, Nijinsky, just like a racehorse, my dad said if he came home and found Colin Bell in bed with the old lady he'd brew him a cup o' tea.

PHIL (*suddenly diverging from the act: no warning*): Look, if you're so funny, why don't you tell us all a joke? (GED *turns his head to look at his brother.*)

GED: You what?

PHIL: Tell us the one about the Pakistani up on a rape charge.

GED (*out of the act, trying to think*): What you talking about?

PHIL (*faintly desperate*): Tell the joke.

(GED *turns his head slowly, stares at the Audience, stands, very slowly, puts his hands on his brother's shoulders, removes him from the stool, takes his place, draws his brother carefully down onto his thigh.*)

GED (*in character*): *You* tell it.

(PHIL *blinks, thinks.*)

44

PHIL (*terrified, struggling for confidence*): This Pakistani, see, up
on a rape charge. So they decide they'll have an identity
parade. They get eight Pakies and they put this one at the
front and explain what they're doing. Then they bring in
the girl and the Pakistani shouts: (*Pakistani voice.*) She's
the one, officer. No doubt about it . . .
(GED *and* PHIL *stare whitely out at the Audience. Neither
knows where to go next.* GED *gets up, repeats the procedure in
reverse until he's back on* PHIL's *knee.*)

GED (*finally*): Shall I sing them a song?

PHIL: Why not?

GED: A song entitled 'If I had it all to do over again, I'd do it
all over you'. How'd you like being the dummy?

PHIL (*a nightmare: wholly dependent on his brother now*): Not a lot.

GED: I thought you were quite good. S'a funny relationship,
innit?

PHIL: How d'you mean?

GED: Well, you know, imagine, you walk in a pub, and there's
this feller having a pint with his hand up the coat of a
little feller sitting on his knee. (*Copper.*) Now then, what
have we here? (*Man, fearful bravado.*) Oh, it's nothing,
officer, we . . . work together . . . er . . . this is how we
always sit. . . . Shall I tell you about the match?

PHIL: Maybe we should sing the song?

GED: Have a look at your watch. (*Two drunk voices.*) Have you
got the right time? Aye, I have. Thanks very much.
(PHIL *looks.*) What's it say?

PHIL: Time for a song.

GED (*back in the act's groove at last*): I'm not going back in that
box after.

PHIL: Sing the song.

GED: All right, but I'm warning you, you *walk* me off, sod your
hernia, I'm not going back in there with her and that
cricket stump . . .

PHIL: Maestro, please.
(PIANIST *plays the intro to the song from the sheet. They share
the line, but gradually double and harmonize, gratefully rather
than well.*)

BOTH: *He's my brother,*
    Our kid
    Don't want another
    Our kid
    He watches over me
    When things get tough
    He pulls the strings
    That wipe the tears away on my cuff . . .
    He's my brother
    Our kid
    And there's no other
    Our kid
    He is my friend, my mate and my mucker
    He's my brother
    Our kid.

(*They stand, take bows and applause, leave.* PIANIST *plays the covering refrain.*)

SECRETARY (*over noise of violent argument from wings; mic.*): Right. (*Pause.*) Another Irishman now—from Belfast this one— good job we kept 'em apart—hands together please for . . . George . . . McBrain.

(MCBRAIN *on, carrying hand-mic. The mania glands sweating freely. He wears a fine maroon evening jacket, hornrimmed glasses on nose end, frills at chest and cuffs of royal blue shirt.*)

MCBRAIN: *In the garden of Eden lay Adam*
    Complacently stroking his madam
    And loud was his mirth
    For he knew that on earth
    There were only two * * *—and he had 'em.

I had a hundred jokes standing back there, I can't remember a one of 'em. (*He looks at the Audience: stares.*) Never mind, I'm good to look at. There's this coloured feller on his way to work. (*Stops.*) Don't you think that's funny? There's this very honest Jew. No favourites here. There's this very brilliant Irishman. From Dublin. I tried to get the wife to come. It gets harder, I dunnit though. I don't say she's jealous but she's the only woman I know. Not a bad pint here, is it. Beats your keg any time, a really well-kept Domestos. You mightn't believe this, but actually I'm from quite a humble background. Me father was humble. Me mother was humble. Very, very humble. (*He's playing the word.*) I was eleven before I stood up. S'true. Used to grovel a lot. Humblest kid in the school. Used to apologize before kicking someone in the head, things like that. I'm still very modest. Mind you, it's a hard fight. (*He shows himself to the ladies in the Audience.*) You can see it, can't you, ladies? (*Sudden thought, hand going down to flies. Mock alarm, controlled.*) Can you? If music be the food of love, how about a bite of your maracas? I was in bed with the wife last Thursday. I said: How about a tongue sandwich before we turn in? I was hungry. *You* get hungry, do you? The wife lay there, very quiet, smoking her pipe. I leaned across and I said or do you fancy anything, Heart? And she said: Yes, I fancy an African about six-foot-three with a big fat . . . cheque book. (*To Audience.*) Don't get ahead of yourselves! Naughty! I said: Yeah? And what do you reckon he'd make of that great fat idle bum of yours? And she said: What makes you think we'd be talking about you? Doesn't say a lot, my wife. Talks all the time but doesn't say a lot. I took her to the zoo. Belle Vue, to see the orang-utan. Enormous. Great painted whatsits, like rump-steak. (*Bunching hands, stomps a bit, pulls the face.*) Like Willy Whitelaw having a shower. She falls right over the wire, as sure as I'm standing here, she trips clean over and lands on her back with her legs parted, her skirt up and her drawers flapping in the wind. I couldn't look, it was horrible. I can remember when I'd a given a week's wages for half what was on show. The big feller kinda sniffs and ambles towards her, and there was this music from his rear end, a slow, tolling, dong, dong, dong. (*Singing.*) The bells of St. Mary's. (*A slow simian swing in perfect time.*) (*Innocent.*) I don't know what caused it. Maybe he'd had one of those suppositories, that gives you music while it works. Anyway . . . he ends up poised above her, like that, and the wife whispers: (*Breathless terror.*) George, what

47

shall I do? What shall I do? And I said: (*Whisper.*) Tell
him you've got a headache . . . Had a look at the alligators.
Just floating handbags really. She's been a goer in her
time, I tell you. Fast? I met her at a dance in Belfast, I
said: Excuse me. She grabbed me by the lapels and stuck
her tongue half-way down me throat. I was only asking for
a light. We had a whirlwind romance, I wined her and
dined her every week for a fortnight, bean soup, pie and
peas, whirlwind. Then I plucked up courage enough to
say the words I never imagined myself saying in a million
years: You're WHAT? And she was. God, what a slut. I
went to see her father . . . out to the Maze prison . . . him
and his six lads all in there together . . . I never saw a
family like it. Ugly? Listen, they wore hoods *before* they
joined the U.V.F., safact. The neighbours made 'em,
protect the kids. First thing he says, You're not a mick,
are you? Certainly not, says I. So why didn't you use
something, says he. Use something? say I. Listen, the first
time I met your daughter she was wearing a notice pinned
to her chest saying I am an epileptic and will die unless
you lie on top of me, there wasn't time for anything like
that. . . . Her mother's as bad. First time she took me
home, the old woman asks me if I'll fetch some coal up
from the cellar. I'm down there two minutes, the wee
daughter arrives to give me a hand or two. Two minutes
later she's picking coal up with the back of her frock—it's
a local custom—the old lady appears at the top of the
stairs, she calls: Daughter, where's your Irish hospitality?
Arch your back, girl, and get that gentleman's equipment
off the cold stone floor. Two kids in the attic talking dirty.
All right, talk dirty, you go first. Hair under your arm.
That's enough. I came. Do you like that? What was I
telling you about? Oh yes, marriage. Seamus got married,
a friend of mine from Cork. (*He gestures big thick 'Irish'.*)
He'd been married about three weeks, he comes to work
rubbing his hands saying: Jesus, did I have a night with
the wife last night. I said three weeks? Why did you wait
so long? He says sure and how was I supposed to know

she was a goer? On the wedding night I said to the wife,
Look, I call this my staff of Infinite Delight. Oh, she says,
I thought it was your Widow's Mite. She's a slut. Wet
dimps in the cups, sinkful of pots, dirty underwear on the
settee and the food, instant pollution. She gave us rabbit
for a fortnight once, every meal. Rabbit pie, rabbit stew,
rabbit rashers, rabbit pâté, rabbit trotters . . . rabbit eggs . . .
After two weeks I was done in, I collapsed holding me
stomach. She said: I'll send for the doctor. I said: Sod the
doctor, see if you can borrow a ferret. I thought of
divorcing her but I don't think there's a court in the
land'd believe me. Anyway, she can be quite nice sometimes.
She looks very good underwater . . . let's face it, few of us
are perfect. Not even the Irish. I was in Belfast the other
week, there's a feller lying out on the pavement with a
bullet hole in his forehead. There's an old lady walks by,
she stops and looks down at yer man for a minute, then she
crosses herself and she says: Well, thank God it missed his
eye. You can't hate 'em can you? Listen, I've gotta go, I'm
wife-swopping tonight. I gorra bloke's greyhound last week,
made a change. So listen, I'll see yer, all right?
(*He takes his bow, sweating, a bit concerned, stiff with tension
now, not looking in* WATERS's *direction.* MCBRAIN *catches*
WATERS's *eye, in a bow: a still moment.* MCBRAIN *breaks,
disappears.*)

SECRETARY (*mic.*): Last, this evening, a young man from Clayton
making his first appearance before an audience, I'm told . . .
a warm hand for . . . Gethin Price.

(PRICE *emerges from the Audience, carrying the tiny violin and
bow. He wears bagging half-mast trousers, large sullen boots,
a red hard wool jersey, studded and battered denim jacket,
sleeves rolled to elbows, a red and white scarf folded at the
neck. His face has been subtly whitened, to deaden and mask
the face. He is half clown, half this year's version of bovver
boy. The effect is calculatedly eerie, funny and chill.*

*He takes out a deeply filthy handkerchief, spreads it carefully,
expertly across his right shoulder, slowly tucks the tiny violin
on his left, stands perfectly still, looks for the first time at the*

Audience. Cocks the bow, stares at it intensely, apparently sinking into process. Notices a very fine thread of gut hanging down. Shakes the bow. Shakes it again. The thread hangs on. He brings the bow finally to his mouth, tries to bite the thread off, his teeth are set on edge, he winces mutely, tries again, can't. He thinks. Tries, bending oddly on one leg, to trap the thread under his huge boot. Fails. Thinks. Puts down the violin at last. Takes out a lighter. Sets fire to the thread. Satisfaction. Puts down the bow. Mimes, in slow motion, Lou Macari running back from his second goal against Burnley in the League Cup, ends up with back to Audience, picks up the violin (in right hand) and bow (in left), meticulously replaces handkerchief on other shoulder. Turns, slow and puzzled, prepares to play. The cocked bow slowly begins to smoulder at the far end. He rams it swiftly into his mouth, removes it fast, mimes a huge silent scream, the quenched bow held upright. Very slowly it begins to crumple. He watches it until it hangs loose in his hand, like a thickish piece of rope. On tape, a piece of intricate Bach for solo violin. Tape ends. He places the spent bow on the stage, puts the violin under his boot, dimps it like a cigarette until it's thoroughly crushed.)

PRICE (*to himself, not admitting the Audience's existence*): I wish I had a train. I feel like smashing a train up. On me own. I feel really strong. Wish I had a train. I could do with some exercise.

(He does a complicated kata, with praying mantis footsweeps, tan-tui, pa-kua dao, and other kung fu exercises. A spot suddenly illuminates dressed dummies of a youngish man and woman: well dressed, beautiful people, a faint, unselfconscious arrogance in their carriage. The man wears evening dress, gloves, etc., the girl a simple, stunning, white full-length dress and fur wrap. Her arm is looped in his. They stand, perhaps waiting for a cab to show after the theatre.

PRICE has continued his exercises throughout this 'arrival'. Becomes aware of them gradually: rises slowly: stares. Turns to the Audience, slowly smiles, evil and childlike. Sniffs. Ambles over. Stands by the man, measuring, walks round to stand by the girl. We sense him being ignored. He begins to

inspect the girl minutely. Finally drops his rattle to the level of her buttocks, lets it rip, harsh, short, opens his eyes wide at the noise, looks covertly down at her arse, steps away from her carefully, scenting the air. Takes a tin from his pocket. Picks from it a badly rolled fag.)
Cigarette? (*Nothing. He offers it to the man.*) No? (*He withdraws the fag, tins it. Looking at them both again, up and down, turns, calls.*) Taxi! (*Sharply, out front, shakes his head as it disappears. Moves round to the man's side again.*) Are you the interpreter then? Been to the match, have we? Were you at t'top end wi' lads? Good, wannit? D'you see Macari? Eh? Eh? (*Silence.*) P'raps I'm not here. Don't you like me? You hardly know me. Let's go and have a pint, get to know each other. Here, don't you live in Salford? I swear I've seen you at the dog track. (*Nothing. He takes a cigarette out of the man's top pocket.*) Very kind of you. Ta. (*He lights the cigarette, blows the smoke in slow separate puffs across the man's face.*) Do you fancy a quick game of crib? (*Very fast.*) Taxi! (*Gone.*) Int this nice? I like a good chat. (*Intimate, man-to-man.*) Eh. I bet she's a goer, int she, sunshine? She's got a fair pair of knockers on her too. Has she been around? Does she ever go dancing at Belle Vue Satdays? I think Eric Yates took her home one night. If it's her, she's a right goer, according to Eric. (*Pause.*) I don't know whether to thump you or what? I suppose I could just give you a clout, just to let you know I exist. (*He blows smoke into the man's face.*) Is that hair dyed? Looks dyed. Are you a puff? Are you a pufter? (*Sniffs; front, fast.*) Taxi! (*Pause.*) That's not a taxi, lady, it's a hearse. (*Evilish grin.*) You're getting confused, lady. Unless you were thinking of getting a quick fun funeral in before retiring for the night. (*To man.*) Say something, Alice? She's calling hearses, he's talking to himself. (*He turns back to the man.*) You do *speak*, do you? I'm trying to *talk* to you. Say some'at. Tell us what kind of day you've had. Are you on the buses? Eh. Shall I make you laugh? This feller pays twenty pounds for this whore, right? Only she dunt fancy him and runs out of the room. He chases her, stark nekkid, down t'street. Cop stops him,

says: Where's the fire, lad? Feller says: I've no idea, but if you see a nude bird running down street, *fuck* her, it's paid for. (*Pause. Nothing.*) You can laugh, you know, I don't mind you laughing. I'm *talking* to you. . . . There's people'd call this *envy*, you know, it's not, it's hate. (*Now very fast.*) Are you bisexual or is that your sister? You'll never get a taxi here, they're all up at Piccadilly waiting for t'last train from London. Ask me how I know. I work there that's why. Don't interrupt when I'm talking, dint your mother ever tell you, it's rude? (*He does a kung fu thrust, missing the man's head by inches.*) Bruce Lee, do you like him? God, he is, you're a stuck-up bastard aren't you? Give us a kiss then, go on, go on, Alice, give us a kiss, I love you. Give us a kiss. (PRICE *halts his burble. Blinks. Pads round to stand at woman's side.*) Say something? (*In her ear.*) Listen . . . I've got a British Rail delivery van round the corner, ditch Alice and we'll do the town. (*He notices a folded copy of* The Times *in the man's hand. Passes behind the figures, pops his head between them.*) Crosswords? (*Thinks a moment.*) Election. Nine across. Big poll in China question mark. (*Chinaman.*) E-lection. (PRICE *looks from one to the other, laughs suddenly. He takes hold of their handles, begins to lift them up and down, to indicate their mirth.*) Election! Election! Big poll in China. Laugh you buggers, laugh! (PRICE *laughs like a drain, throws himself around the stage, cartwheels and rolls mixed in with elaborate tai-chi gestures. Eventually he subsides, returns.*) Yeah. Here. (*He takes a flower out of his pocket, hands it out to the man.*) For the lady. Here's a pin. (*Pause.*) I'll do it, shall I? (*He pins the flower—a marigold— with the greatest delicacy between the girl's breasts. Steps back to look at his work.*) No need for thanks. My pleasure entirely. Believe me. (*Silence. Nothing. Then a dark red stain, rapidly widening, begins to form behind the flower.*) Aagh, aagh, aagh, aagh . . .
(*The spot fades slowly on the cut-outs, centring finally on the red stain.* PRICE's '*aaghs*' *become short barks of laughter.*)
(*Innocence.*) I wonder what happened. P'raps it pierced a vein.

(*Their light goes altogether. We're left with his single, chill image.*)

I made him laugh though. (*Depressed.*) Who needs *them*? Hunh. Who needs them? We manage. Uni-ted. Uni-ted. Docherty, Docherty. You won't keep us down with the tiddlers, don't worry. We're coming up *there* where we can gerrat yer. (*Sings.*) Lou Macari, Lou Macari. . . . I shoulda smashed him. They allus mek you feel sorry for 'em, out in the open. I suppose I shoulda just kicked him without looking at him. (*Pause. He looks after them. Calling.*) National Unity? Up yours, sunshine. (*Pause. He picks up the tiny violin, i.e. another, switched, uncrushed, and a bow. Addresses it. Plays 'The Red Flag', very simple and direct, four bars.*) Still. I made the buggers laugh . . .

(*He walks off. The concert* SECRETARY, *probably shocked, embarrassed, not wishing to dwell. Lights fade.* WATERS *stands, face gaunt, grey.* CHALLENOR *tosses off a scotch, sheafs his notes, pockets pen.*)

SECRETARY: That's the lot, ladies and gentlemen, you have your cards, I think, Charlie Shaw has 'em for them that hasn't, and we're starting right away, settle yourselves down now. And it's eyes down for a full house . . . (*Lights fade gradually.*) Allus look after . . . Number One. (*Lights fade to black.*)

ACT THREE

Classroom. Time: 9.43. Empty.

MCBRAIN, SAMUELS *and* CONNOR *return slowly, to sit in their respective places, though an almost deliberate distance apart.* PHIL MURRAY *in. They sit, glum, drained, separate.*

Simple exhaustion underpins the low, tense, anxious, angry, baffled mood of the four. No eye contacts. People sit or fiddle. SAMUELS *sits in his coat, ready for away.* CONNOR *is again pretty wet.* MCBRAIN *has changed back to his parka and jeans, his bag on the desk in front of him.*

PRICE, *off, suddenly starts up with 'There's no business like show business . . .'*

PHIL: Listen to that stupid cunt.

SAMUELS: There'll be no pigging business for *him*, that's for a certainty. Did you ever see owt like it? He's bloody puddled. (PRICE *in, dressed as in Act One: smells the mood of the others; dwells for a moment in the doorway.*)

MCBRAIN: Did you see that Challenor feller? He smiled twice all evening, and both times it was at some'at the sodding concert secretary said.

CONNOR (*low*): I don't reckon it was much fun for Mr. Waters either.

PHIL (*checking door with a look*): Look, sod Mr. Waters. He's not handing jobs out, is he, Seamus?

CONNOR (*dangerous, suddenly, very deliberate*): My name's Mick. (*Silence.*)

MCBRAIN: Take it easy, Michael . . .

CONNOR (*ignoring him*): Mick.

PHIL: All right. Mick.

(GED MURRAY *has appeared wet through in the doorway, in*

54

time for the last exchange.)

GED (*finally*): Fish and chips. It's teeming down.

MCBRAIN: About bloody time. Did you nip home to make 'em?

GED (*giving them out*): Ha bloody ha. There was a queue a mile long. It's next t'British Legion, innit. (*He's with* SAMUELS.) They dint have any silver hake. I got you a pie.

SAMUELS: A pie? What d'you get a pie for?

GED (*handing it to him*): I thought you might be hungry.

SAMUELS (*opening package*): A pie? I don't eat pies.

(GED *moves back towards his seat, taking in* PRICE *with a wave on the way back.*)

GED (*to* PRICE): Hey, that was great, Geth . . .

(PRICE *winks.*)

MCBRAIN: They're stone bloody cold.

GED (*on way*): It's a long bloody way.

SAMUELS (*staring at the pie he's broken*): It's a bloody *pork* pie!

GED: Is it? Don't you like pork?

SAMUELS: God almighty, I ask for silver hake, he brings us a pork pie . . .

PRICE (*about dressed, approaching: Revivalist voice*): Holy pig. Here, give us it here.

(*He takes the pie, carries it over to the desks.*

GED *moves to* PRICE's *chair very deliberately, passing his own on the way, sits facing out, his back to his brother:* PHIL *stares at* GED *with hostility.* PRICE *notes the change in seating, takes up the centre position between them, stands for a moment, leaning on the chairback, regards the other five very carefully for a moment without speaking.*)

Dearly beloved, we are gathered here in the sight of Mammon to mourn the passing of several very promising careers in the comedic arts. For those who live on . . . the words of the great and holy musical *The Song of Norway* will be of special comfort: De cuntibus minibus tuum, rectum anus mirabilis est. Which loosely translated means: It's easy to be a bit of a cunt, you've got to work to become a shithouse. Here endeth lesson one. (*He blesses them gravely, sits down.*)

(*Silence.*)

SAMUELS (*finally, ugly*): You got anyone . . . special in mind, Charlie?

(PRICE *gets up swiftly, crosses to the dais, picks up a chair leg left by the* CARETAKER, *holds it in two hands a foot or so from his forehead, breathes very deeply three or four times, then smashes it cleanly with his forehead. He carries the two ends to* SAMUELS, *puts them carefully on his desk.*)

PRICE: Build yourself a cross, Sammy. You're gonna crucify the man, do the job properly.

(*He turns, walks away, resumes his seat.* SAMUELS *grasps the two ends,* MCBRAIN *takes them from him with gentle power, carries them to the waste paper basket.*)

MCBRAIN: There was this feller, see . . .

CONNOR (*fraying*): No more jokes, George. All right?

(MCBRAIN *deposits the ends, returns to his seat. Silence.* GED *finishes his chips, wipes his hands on the paper.*)

GED (*casual, innocent, knowing*): You'll be all right, George. You knew what to do all right.

MCBRAIN (*a freak of anger at the vent*): So when do I get the thirty pieces of silver? (*He bangs the desk with his fist, a harsh, half-self-punishing gesture.*) I don't want inquests, I want work.

SAMUELS: Right! Who the fuck does he (PRICE) think he is anyway! (*To* PRICE.) What about your . . . performance then, Coco the bloody clown? It was bloody embarrassing . . .

GED: It were different.

SAMUELS: Different? It was putrid. Different from bloody comedy, that's for sure.

CONNOR: Look, for Jesus Christ's sake, it's over, will you forget it . . .

GED: Hey, *you* were good, Mick, what I could hear of it. You got most of 'em in too, dint you.

CONNOR: Yeah. I went down like a fart at a funeral.

PHIL: What a bleeding audience. Thick as pig shit.

PRICE: A bad lover blames his tool.

SAMUELS: So why didn't the great Lancashire Lad do a warm-up then, eh? He sent you out cold, and I had to follow you.

GED: Oh, *you* found your feet all right, Sammy . . . .

SAMUELS: What does that mean then?

(*The* CARETAKER *comes in, a large battery lamp in his hand.*)

CARETAKER: You lot still here? I'm waiting to lock up you know. I've got a home to go to. Somebody left that thing . . . (*He points to the muslin sack.*) . . . Meat.

(*He leaves, turning into* WATERS.)

WATERS: We won't be long now . . .

CARETAKER: I hope not. I'm not on overtime you know . . .

(*He leaves.* WATERS *stands a moment in the doorway looking into the room. They stare, some of them half-turning, at him. He's white, drained, tired and old. He walks, less spryly, to the desk. Sits down. Stares at the desk top. Silence. Some looks round the room.*)

GED (*holding them up*): There's a packet of chips if you want them, Mr. Waters.

(WATERS *looks at him, makes no answer.* CHALLENOR *in, shaking his coat.*)

CHALLENOR: Sorry, gentlemen. Several calls of nature on the way. You won't have reached your prostates yet, but you will. Mind if I use the desk, Eddie?

(WATERS *relinquishes the desk, goes to lean by the windows, an onlooker.* CHALLENOR *places his case down, opens it, removes notes and forms, flicks through them, sniffs. Looks at* PRICE *covertly once or twice. Gathers.*)

Right, there's not much time, so I'll get cracking. Interesting evening. Lot of promise. I'll take you one by one so we don't get mixed up. Mick Connor.

CONNOR: Yeah.

CHALLENOR: Aye. You've not done a lot, have you?

CONNOR: No, I've done nothing. Concerts, works do's.

CHALLENOR: I quite liked it. One or two quite nice jokes, quite nicely told. (*Studying notes.*) Bit old-fashioned. I thought, you know, following a single topic through your act. It mighta worked even so, if you'd taken something more up the audience's street. I mean, you might find being an Irishman in England fascinating, there's no reason we should, is there? (*Pause.*) Had a sort of . . . earnestness about it I didn't much take to. You know, as if you were

57

giving a sermon. One thing you've gotta learn, people don't learn, they don't want to, and if they did, they won't look to the likes of us to teach 'em. You've got to be very good indeed to patronize your audience, I can tell you. (*Pause.*) The sex was crude. I've nothing against it, but it requires taste, if you see what I mean, I've never heard a good joke yet about coitus interruptus. Still, you had your moments. Some promise there. (*Turns* CONNOR's *sheet onto its face.*) Sammy Samuels?

SAMUELS: Himself.

CHALLENOR: I thought you'd never get started. First thing you want to do is ditch the first half of your act.

SAMUELS: Yeah, it's stuff I've been shedding, you know . . .

CHALLENOR: S'too Jewish. What's a Jew nowadays εh? Who wants to know I mean.

SAMUELS: Yeah, I can see that.

CHALLENOR: Same mistake as the Irishman. (*Looks at notes.*) Fortunately, you pulled out of it and got very good. It was a different act, the wife, blacks, Irish, women, you spread it around, you can score, keep it tight they'll fall asleep on you. (*Pause.*) Liked the Women's Lib bits. (*Pause.*) You need an ending, you were just sticking one after another till you'd done. No climax. People want a climax.

SAMUELS: Yeah, I er . . . got off the rails a bit actually . . .

CHALLENOR: Stay on 'em. Phil and Ged Murray.

PHIL: Here.

CHALLENOR: Aye well, what went wrong there? (PHIL *and* GED *look at each other briefly.*) There was a distinct smell of cock-up on the air about half-way through (*Reading notes.*) I've got a note about a Pakistani on a rape charge . . . Aye, that's it. What happened then?
(PHIL *looks at* GED. *Finally.*)

GED (*very quietly*): We got lost.

CHALLENOR: What, was it new material or something?

GED: Yeah. Something like that.

CHALLENOR: Well it was horrible. The cardinal sin for any performer is embarrassing the audience. *You* had 'em doing up their shoelaces and picking up old beer mats.

(*Pause.*) I don't know. It's a nice idea, but you need the material, my God, if you're gonna carry it off.

GED: We missed a lot out, after we got lost.

CHALLENOR (*interest faded*): I'm sure you did. I'm sure you did. Liked the song, nice sentiment. Quite catchy really . . .
(*He slashes his pencil across their page of notes, turns over.*)
George McBrain. (MCBRAIN *shows.*) Cracking opening. Bang. No messing. Liked it. Lot of sex but well handled, if you see what I mean. Near the knuckle but not half-way up the armpit. A question of taste. Knowing when to draw back. Even with yobboes like that lot down there. (*Pause.*) Quite subtle but not too subtle. 'Tell *him* you've gotta headache . . .' 'Floating handbags' . . . Yes, yes . . . Good character, I believed it, it was all of a piece. Confident, a bit aggressive, like that. Like the joke about the thick Seamus. (*To* CONNOR.) See, that's what I mean, don't push your own particular prejudice, you're there on *their* terms, not your own. (*Notes again.*) Good ending. (*Nodding in* SAMUELS'S *direction.*) See, it was *down*beat, but it was firm. You know, diminuendo. Well thought out . . .
(*There's a long pause now, as he stares at* PRICE'S *notes. People make sweating faces on their own chances.* WATERS *leans, half sits, against the window, staring nowhere, withdrawn, remote.* PRICE *leans almost horizontally back in his chair, staring at the ceiling. He remains like this throughout most of the following.*)
(*Finally.*) Gethin Price. (*Another pause.*) Mmmmmmm. Mmmmmmm. (*Looks across at* PRICE *finally, no nonsense, man to man . . .* PRICE *is about to levitate.* CHALLENOR *looks in* WATERS'S *direction, seeking guidance.* WATERS *purses his lips, looks out of the window.*) Not a lot to say about your piece, Price. You have a certain talent maybe as a mime, something like that. . . . What you did tonight just . . . won't do. Music hall maybe, but there *is* no music hall. . . . You wanna be a comedian, you'd better start somewhere else, there's no way you'll get started with what you've got. Not viable. You've got to speak to the audience, for God's sake. (*Pause. Studying notes.*) Personally, I found the content

59

of your act . . . how shall I put it? . . . repulsive. (*He stares on at his notes.* PRICE *slowly resumes an upright position in the chair.*) And aggressively unfunny. (*He looks at* PRICE, *practisedly kindly.*) If you want to get on, lad, you'd better sort a few problems out first. Get some distance, see what I mean. Don't give us your hang-ups straight. Too hot to handle. (*Closes note-file decisively.*) Four golden rules. For all of you, though some more than others. One. All audiences are thick, collectively, but it's a bad comedian who lets 'em know it. Two. Two laughs are better than one. Always. Three. You don't have to love the people, but the people *have* to love you. Four. Sell yourself. If you're giving it away, it won't be worth having. (*Pause.*) All right, I coulda left this till I got back south, but I'm not that sorta person. At the moment, on tonight, I'm interested in just two of you . . . you (MCBRAIN) and you (SAMUELS) . . . I've got forms here (*Holds them up.*) . . . enrolment. When these've been received, there'll be an agent to look after your business and develop your career. Don't give your jobs up just now, mind. There'll be time enough for that when you're getting the bookings. (*He gives forms to* MCBRAIN *and* SAMUELS.) For the rest of you, I'll see you again. Drop me a line, I'm approachable. Just as long as you've learnt your lessons from tonight, that is. It's not the talent's lacking; it's application of a few basic rules of professional life. (*Turns to* WATERS.) Thanks, Eddie. Nice evening. Some good lads. Few wild notions mebbe but . . .

(WATERS *walks towards him, takes the proffered hand.*)

I'm down at the Midland. How about a drink?

WATERS: Still full of shit, Bert. Fuller than a large intestine.

CHALLENOR: How's that, Eddie?

WATERS: You wouldn't know a comedian from a barrowload of crap.

CHALLENOR (*light, unruffled*): Meaning you disagree. Oh. Send in a report.

WATERS: I don't belong, remember?

CHALLENOR: What do you expect? A hundred per cent?

WATERS: They were nobbled, Bert. They're great lads.

CHALLENOR: Your opinion. Don't be ungracious . . .

WATERS: Yeah. Enjoy the Midland.

CHALLENOR (*smiling evenly*): Always do, Eddie. *Like* the best.
(*He picks up his briefcase, leaves with what dignity he can
salvage. A deep, uneasy silence.* PRICE *tosses and catches the
pork pie, rhythmically like a juggler.*)

PRICE (*without venom*): There goes nothing. A man who doesn't
rate Frank Randle, what does *he* know?

WATERS (*deliberately*): He knows enough, Mr. Price. He knows
where the door marked In is.

PRICE: Yeah, but you know where it leads? (*Looking at* MCBRAIN
and SAMUELS.) It leads to a room with a notice on the wall
and the notice says 'Kindly ensure that you leave this room
as you found it'. A shitheap.

MCBRAIN: No need to be bitter, Geth. You'll make out . . .
(PRICE *laughs, hard, unpleasant, remote.*)

PRICE (*perfect Ulster*): Thanks, George. S'very good of you.
Just you remember now—stand you your ground.
(MCBRAIN *stands up, a little uncertainly. Picks up the bag.*)

MCBRAIN: A comic's a comic's a comic. Ain't that right though.
(*Sniff. Pause.*) Thanks, Mr. Waters. It's been a great great
pleasure. I'll never forget what you've done for me . . .

WATERS (*with effort*): Yes. Enjoy yourself, George. I'll watch out
for you.

MCBRAIN: We'll have a drink sometime.

WATERS: Yes.

MCBRAIN: Look after yourself. (*Turning.*) And you lot.
Scrubbers. (*Going.*)

SAMUELS (*standing*): Hang on, George. I'll give you a lift, we
can stop off at the club for a drink.

MCBRAIN: No good, Sammy. I'm late as it is. The wife's not
bin too good lately . . . I'd best get off.

SAMUELS: She'll not begrudge you a celebration pint, surely to
God?

MCBRAIN (*steel suddenly*): She begrudges me nothing, Sammy.
(*Small silence. He leaves, kiln-fired, hard inside the
compromise.*)

61

SAMUELS: How about you, Phil? (PHIL *shakes his head whitely.*)
Well . . . Cheers, Mr. Waters. A pleasure to know you.
(*Offers hand.*)

WATERS (*taking it*): Aye.

SAMUELS: Hard work, by Christ. Lost me script completely
tonight. Don't know how I kept going . . .

WATERS: No.

SAMUELS: Couldn'ta done it without you, Mr. Waters, that's for
a certainty.
(*He treks the lonely walk to the door. Leaves. Everyone stands,
preparing to go.* PHIL MURRAY *suddenly stands, lifts his bag,
slams it down on the desk.*)

PHIL (*to* GED, *smouldering*): You coming?

GED (*turning slowly*): No. I'll catch a bus.

PHIL: It's pissing down.

GED: Yeah well . . . I need the air.

PHIL (*vicious*): Suit yourself.
(*He turns to leave. Turns back again.*)
Are you going up the Infirmary Sunday?

GED: Yeah. Why?

PHIL (*pulls a quid out of his back pocket, hands it to* GED): Give
him this will you? Some fags or some'at. Tell him I'll . . .
try and make it week after.
(GED *takes the note.* PHIL *leaves.*)

CONNOR (*approaching* WATERS's *desk*): Sorry if we let you down.

WATERS: Not you, son. Not in a million years. Stay that way.
Because that way is a good way.
(*He holds his hand out.* CONNOR *takes it.*)
I'm . . . sorry.

CONNOR (*soft*): Get stuffed.
(CONNOR *winks at* PRICE *and* GED MURRAY, *leaves briskly,
stops suddenly in the doorway.*)
Shit! I never told me copper joke! I've been working on it
all week . . . (*He bangs his temple with his palm several
times.*) Dummy, dummy.
(*He's gone.*)

GED: Anyone fancy a pint? I fancy a pint. Or seven. Better get
me skates on. (*He crosses to* WATERS.) Will there be . . . will

62

you be doing this again another time, Mr. Waters?

WATERS: Yes, I've a few lads lined up starting May . . .

GED: I'd like to come back, if you'd have me.

WATERS: No no. You need to *do* it now, Ged. You *have* it, lad. Believe that.

GED: Mebbe, mebbe not. I wanna go solo, see. (*Exchanges look with* PRICE.) That cock-up . . . it weren't nerves, it weren't . . . technique . . . it were deliberate. (*Pointing at door.*) Him. He wanted to put some'at in for Challenor. I wouldn't have it. (*Grins, sniffs.*) I thought I were going reet well up to then. Felt good too.

WATERS: Remember it, how it feels when it's good. It's important. (*Holds hand out.*) Good-night. I'll see you soon.

GED (*embarrassed*): Oh, I nearly forgot. Erm. (*Small package from pocket.*) We . . . er . . . we clubbed together some of us and bought you this. (*He hands him the package, smiles, leaves.*)

(*In the corridor we hear the* CARETAKER *quizzing* GED.)

CARETAKER (*off*): It's not a bloody all-night session is it? Because if it is I'm on the bloody phone to Nalgo right away . . .

(WATERS *unwraps the package. It's a pipe.* WATERS *studies it.*)

PRICE: No one . . . clubbed together.

WATERS (*gravely*): That's all right. I don't smoke either.

(WATERS *begins to pack his things, put on his overcoat, etc.* PRICE *watches him, fascinated.*)

I don't know what to say, Gethin. It's late. Maybe you shouldn't ask. It's been a funny night all round. (*He waves towards the door. Pause.*) And you. You've always been a bit wild, it's why I liked you, reminded me of me at twenty-five. Tonight . . . (*He leaves it, fastens his bag.*) I don't know . . .

PRICE: Did you like what I did? I'm asking.

WATERS: Like? (*Pause.*) It was terrifying.

PRICE: You know what they did, don't you?

WATERS: Oh yes.

PRICE: Do you blame 'em?

WATERS (*emphatic*): No. We make our own beds.

PRICE (*angry suddenly*): I didn't sell you out, Eddie.

(WATERS *frowns, turns slowly, straightening, to face* PRICE.)

63

WATERS: Is that what you think I think?

PRICE: Samuels, McBrain, they're nothing. They'll just float through the system like turds on the Irwell, they sold out because they've nothing worth holding on to. You can't blame them for doing it any more than you can praise Connor and Ged Murray for not. They stayed put because they've nowhere else to go . . .

WATERS: Listen, don't go on, we'll talk again . . .

PRICE: I just wanted it to be *me* talking out there. I didn't want to do something *we*'d worked on. You know.

WATERS (*lifting very suddenly, disturbed*): Look, I *saw* it, you don't have to tell me what I already know . . .

PRICE: I want you to see the *difference* . . .

WATERS (*shouting*) . . . I *see* the difference. God Almighty, I see it, I see it, I just . . . don't understand it.

PRICE (*shouting*): Well then why don't you listen to what I'm *saying*, Eddie?

(*Silence.* WATERS *looks at the clock.*)

WATERS: All right.

(*Pause.*)

PRICE (*quiet*): I can't paint *your* pictures. (*Points to eyes.*) These see.

WATERS: It's not only what you see, it's what you feel when you see it . . .

PRICE: What *I* feel. *I* feel.

WATERS: No compassion, no truth. You threw it all out, Gethin. Love, care, concern, call it what you like, you junked it over the side.

PRICE: I didn't junk it. It was never there . . .

WATERS: What're you talking about . . .?

PRICE: . . . you're avoiding the question, Eddie.

WATERS: I don't know what to say . . .

PRICE: . . . Was I good or was I crap . . .?

WATERS (*loud, compelled*): . . . You were *brilliant*!

(*Pause.* PRICE *blinks.* WATERS *glowers at the new terrain.*)

PRICE (*slowly*): But you . . . didn't like it.

(WATERS *shakes his head.*)

(*Soft, slow.*) Why not?

64

WATERS (*eventually*): It was ugly. It was drowning in hate. You
can't change today into tomorrow on that basis. You
forget a thing called . . . the truth.

PRICE: The truth. Can I say . . . look, I wanna say something.
What do you know about the *truth*, Mr. Waters? You think
the truth is *beautiful*? You've forgotten what it's *like*.
You knew it when you started off, Oldham Empire, People's
Music Hall, Colne Hippodrome, Bolton Grand, New
Brighton Palace, Ardwick Empire, Ardwick Hippodrome,
the Met, the Star in Ancoats . . . the Lancashire Lad—you
knew it then all right. Nobody hit harder than Eddie
Waters, that's what they say. Because you were still in
touch with what made you . . . hunger, diphtheria, filth,
unemployment, penny clubs, means tests, bed bugs, head
lice. . . . Was all *that* truth beautiful? (*Pause.* WATERS *stares
at him, blinded.*) Truth was a fist you hit with. Now it's
like . . . now it's like cowflop, a day old, hard until it's
underfoot and then it's . . . green, soft. Shitten. (*Pause.*)
Nothing's changed, Mr. Waters, is what I'm saying. When
I stand upright—like tonight at that club—I bang my head
on the ceiling. Just like you fifty years ago. We're still
caged, exploited, prodded and pulled at, milked, fattened,
slaughtered, cut up, fed out. We still don't belong to
ourselves. Nothing's changed. You've just forgotten, that's
all.
(WATERS *gathers his things about him, using the process.*)
And you . . . stopped laughing, didn't you? Not even a
warm-up tonight. You had nothing to say to those people
down there tonight, did you?
(WATERS *turns slowly to face him.*)
In three months or more, you never said a single funny
thing. (*Pause.*) Challenor reckons you could have been great
. . . he said you just stopped wanting it.
(WATERS *sits down heavily at the desk, the pain hurting now.*)
Maybe you lost your hate, Mr. Waters.

WATERS (*fierce*): What are you, twenty-five, twenty-six?

PRICE: What?

WATERS: Before you were born, I was touring with E.N.S.A.,

the war had just ended, a year, maybe more. We were in Germany, B.A.O.R., fooling about till we got our blighty bonds. Somebody . . . somebody said there was a guided tour of a bit of East Germany on offer, I got a ticket. I saw Dresden. Dresden? Twenty-five miles of rubble. Freddie Tarleton was with us, good comic, he said it reminded him of Ancoats. . . . Then they took us to a place called Weimar, where Mozart had a house. Saw his work room, his desk, piano, books. These perfect rooms, all over the house, the sun on the windows. . . . Down the road, four miles maybe, we pulled up at this camp. There was a party of schoolkids getting down off a truck ahead of us. And we followed 'em in. It was Buchenwald. 'To each his own' over the gate. They'd cleaned it up, it was like a museum, each room with its separate, special collection. In one of 'em . . . the showers . . . there was a box of cyanide pellets on a table. 'Ciankali' the label said, just that. A block away, the incinerators, with a big proud maker's label moulded on its middle, someone in Hamburg. . . . And then this extraordinary thing. (*Longish pause.*) In this hell-place, a special block, 'Der Straf-bloc', 'Punishment Block'. It took a minute to register, I almost laughed, it seemed so ludicrous. Then I saw it. It was a world like any other. It was the logic of our world . . . extended . . . (*Pulling out of the deep involvement phase of the story.*) We crossed back into West Germany the same night, Freddie was doing a concert in Bielefeld. (*Long pause.*) And he . . . quite normally, he's going along, getting the laughs, he tells this joke about a Jew . . . I don't remember what it was . . . I don't remember what it was . . . people laughed, not inordinately, just . . . easily . . . And I sat there. And I didn't laugh.

(*He stands suddenly. Looks hard at* PRICE.)
That exercise we do . . . thinking of something deep, personal, serious . . . then being funny about it . . . That's where it came from. (*Long pause.*) And I discovered . . . there were no jokes left. Every joke was a little pellet, a . . . final solution. We're the only animal that laughs. The only

66

one. You know when you see the chimpanzees on the PG Tips things snickering, do you know what that is? Fear. They're signalling their terror. We've gotta do some'at about it, Gethin.

PRICE: Did you learn to love the Nazis then . . . (*He says it with soft z, as in Churchill.*)

WATERS: . . . I'm not saying *that* . . .

PRICE: . . . That's what I'm *hearing* . . .

WATERS: . . . It's not as simple . . .

PRICE: . . . It's simple to me . . .

WATERS: . . . It wasn't only repulsive . . .

PRICE: What else was it then . . .?

WATERS (*wrenched from him, finally*): I got an erection in that . . . place! An erection! Gethin. Something . . . (*He touches his stomach.*) . . . loved it, too. (*Silence.* PRICE *turns away from* WATERS, *takes two precise paces towards the back of the room, turns back again.*) We've gotta get deeper than hate. Hate's no help.

PRICE: A German joke is no laughing matter.

WATERS: See it.

(PRICE *turns away again, prods the muslin sack with his boot.*)

PRICE: I found it in the book you lent me. The idea for the act.

WATERS: It was Grock. I worked with him once.

PRICE: It was Grock. Thing I liked was his . . . hardness. Not like Chaplin, all coy and covered in kids. This book said he weren't even funny. He was just very truthful, everything he did. (*He fiddles in his pocket, takes out some paper, etc. Finds the piece of paper he's looking for, opens it.*) I found this in another book. I brought it to show you. Some say the world will end in fire. Some say in ice. From what I've tasted of desire I hold with those who favour fire, but if I had to perish twice, I think I know enough of hate to say that for destruction ice is also great and would suffice. (*He folds the paper, puts it back in his pocket, moves to desk, picks up his bag, rather casually.*) It was all ice out there tonight. I loved it. I felt . . .

expressed. (*Pause. lifting suddenly.*) The Jews still stayed
in line, even when they *knew*, Eddie! What's *that* about?
(*He swings his bag off the desk, ready for off.*)
I stand in no line. I refuse my consent.
(*Pause.* WATERS *fastens his coat collar.*)

WATERS (*very quiet*): What do you do now then?

PRICE: I go back. I wait. I'm ready.

WATERS: Driving, you mean?

PRICE: Driving. It doesn't matter.

WATERS: Wait for what?

PRICE: Wait for it to happen.

WATERS (*very low*): Do you want help?

PRICE: No. I'm OK. Watch out for me.

WATERS: How's Margaret?

PRICE (*plain*): She left. Took the kiddie. Gone to her sister's in
Bolton.

WATERS (*finally*): I'm sorry.

PRICE: It's nothing. I cope. (*Pause.*) What do you do then?
Carry on with this?

WATERS: I don't know.

PRICE: You should. You do it well.

(*They stay a moment longer, perhaps pondering a handshake.*
PRICE *turns, leaves.*

   WATERS *sits on at the desk, his back half-turned to the door.*
After a moment, PATEL *arrives, knocks on the open door.*
WATERS *stands without turning.*)

WATERS (*as though to* CARETAKER): All right, I'm on my way . . .

PATEL: Please, I left this parcel . . .

WATERS (*turning, standing*): So you did. Not been your night,
has it. Me too.

(PATEL *smiles, humps the sack under his arm.*)

WATERS: What's in there, anyway?

PATEL: Some beef. A big piece. I work at abattoir.

WATERS: Y'eat beef do you then?

PATEL: No, no, I'm Hindu. Beef, cow is sacred. This is for a
friend.

WATERS: Oh. (*Pause.*) Don't you mind . . . handling it?

PATEL: At first. Not now. (*He puts the sack down, stares around the desk.*) All your funny men have gone home?

WATERS: Yeah. All the funny men have gone home.

PATEL: You like to hear a joke from my country?

WATERS (*frowning*): Try me.

PATEL (*laughing, excited*): It's very funny, it's very, very funny. A man has many children, wife, in the South. His crop fail, he have nothing, the skin shrivel on his children's ribs, his wife's milk dries. They lie outside the house starving. All around them, the sacred cows, ten, twenty, more, eating grass. One day he take sharp knife, mm? He creep up on a big white cow, just as he lift knife the cow see him and the cow say, Hey, aren't you knowing you not permitted to kill me? And the man say, What do you know, a talking horse. (PATEL *laughs a lot.* WATERS *suddenly begins to laugh too.* PATEL *lifts the sack again.*)

WATERS: What do you know, a talking horse. That's Jewish. It is. Come on, I'll give you a lift. Listen, I'm starting another class in May, why don't you join it? You might enjoy it . . . (*They leave the room.* WATERS *snicks off the lights, one pair, two. The room is lit by corridor lighting only now. We hear shouted goodnights, the clanking of keys, the banging of a pair of doors. A torch light flashes into the room through the corridor window and the* CARETAKER *arrives for a final check. He flashes the light round the room, teacher's desk, desks, dais, blackboard. The beam picks out the scrawled radiograph of* PRICE's *limerick: Pratt (Twat), etc.*)

CARETAKER (*finally, with considerable sourness*): The dirty buggers.

(*He crosses, fishes out a rag, begins to wipe it away.*)

Selected List of Grove Press Drama and Theater Paperbacks

E487   ABE, KOBE / Friends / $2.45

E449   ARDEN, JOHN / Armstrong's Last Goodnight / $1.50

E412   ARDEN, JOHN / The Business of Good Government: A Christmas Play / $1.45

E404   ARDEN, JOHN / Left-Handed Liberty: A Play About Magna Carta / $2.45

E312   ARDEN, JOHN / Serjeant Musgrave's Dance / $2.45 [See also Modern British Drama, Henry Popkin, ed. GT614 / $5.95]

B109   ARDEN, JOHN / Three Plays: Live Like Pigs, The Waters of Babylon, The Happy Haven / $2.45

E610   ARRABAL, FERNANDO / And They Put Handcuffs on The Flowers / $1.95

E486   ARRABAL, FERNANDO / The Architect and The Emperor of Assyria / $2.40

E611   ARRABAL, FERNANDO / Garden of Delights / $2.95

E521   ARRABAL, FERNANDO / Guernica and Other Plays (The Labyrinth, The Tricycle, Picnic on the Battlefield) / $2.45

E532   ARTAUD, ANTONIN / The Cenci / $1.95

E127   ARTAUD, ANTONIN / The Theater and Its Double (Critical Study) / $2.95

E425   BARAKA, IMAMU AMIRI (LEROI JONES) / The Baptism and The Toilet / $2.45

E540   BARNES, PETER / The Ruling Class / $2.95

E471   BECKETT, SAMUEL / Cascando and Other Short Dramatic Pieces (Words and Music, Film, Play, Come and Go, Eh Joe, Endgame) / $1.95

E96   BECKETT, SAMUEL / Endgame / $1.95

E318   BECKETT, SAMUEL / Happy Days / $2.45

E226   BECKETT, SAMUEL / Krapp's Last Tape, plus All That Fall, Embers, Act Without Words I and II / $2.45

E33   BECKETT, SAMUEL / Waiting For Godot / $1.95 [See also Seven Plays of the Modern Theater, Harold Clurman, ed. GT422 / $4.95]

B79   BEHAN, BRENDAN / The Quare Fellow* and The Hostage**: Two Plays / $2.45 *[See also Seven Plays of the Modern Theater, Harold Clurman, ed. GT422 / $4.95] **[See also Modern British Drama, Henry Popkin, ed. GT614 / $5.95]

E624   BEHAN, BRENDAN / Richard's Cork Leg / $2.95

E534   BENTLEY, ERIC / A Time to Die and A Time to Live: Two Short Plays / $1.95

GT423 BOWERS, FAUBIAN / Theatre in the East: A Survey of Asian Dance and Drama / $3.95

B117   BRECHT, BERTOLT / The Good Woman of Setzuan / $1.95

B80   BRECHT, BERTOLT / The Jewish Wife and Other Short Plays (In Search of Justice, The Informer, The Elephant Calf, The Measures Taken, The Exception and the Rule, Salzburg Dance of Death) / $1.65

B90   BRECHT, BERTOLT / The Mother / $1.45

B108   BRECHT, BERTOLT / Mother Courage and Her Children / $1.50

B333   BRECHT, BERTOLT / The Threepenny Opera / $1.45

B88   BRECHT, BERTOLT / The Visions of Simone Machard / $1.25

E517   BULGAKOV, MIKHAIL / Flight: A Play in Eight Dreams and Four Acts / $2.25

E520   COE, RICHARD N. (Ed.) / The Theater of Jean Genet: A Casebook / $3.95

E441   COHN, RUBY (Ed.) / Casebook on Waiting for Godot / $3.95

E581   CESAIRE, AIME / A Season in the Congo / $2.45

GT422 CLURMAN, HAROLD (Ed.) / Seven Plays of the Modern Theater / $4.95 (Waiting For Godot by Samuel Beckett, The Quare Fellow by Brendan Behan, A Taste of Honey by Shelagh Delaney, The Connection by Jack Gelber, The Balcony by Jean Genet, Rhinoceros by Eugene Ionesco, and The Birthday Party by Harold Pinter)

E159   DELANEY, SHELAGH / A Taste of Honey / $1.95 (See also Modern British Drama, Henry Popkin, ed., GT614 / $5.95, and Seven Plays of the Modern Theater, Harold Clurman, ed. GT422 / $4.95)

E402   DURRENMATT, FRIEDRICH / An Angel Comes to Babylon and Romulus the Great / $3.95

E401   DURRENMATT, FRIEDRICH / The Marriage of Mr. Mississippi and Problems of the Theatre (Play and Essay) / $3.95

E628   DURRENMATT, FRIEDRICH / The Meteor / $1.95

E380   DURRENMATT, FRIEDRICH / The Physicists / $2.95

E612   DURRENMATT, FRIEDRICH / Play Strindberg / $1.95

E344   DURRENMATT, FRIEDRICH / The Visit / $2.75

B215   DYER, CHARLES / Staircase / $1.95

B132   GARSON, BARBARA / MacBird! / $1.95

E223   GELBER, JACK / The Connection / $2.45 [See also Seven Plays of the Modern Theater, Harold Clurman, ed. GT422 / $4.95]

E130   GENET, JEAN / The Balcony / $2.95 [See also Seven Plays of the Modern Theater, Harold Clurman, ed. GT422 / $4.95]

E208   GENET, JEAN / The Blacks: A Clown Show / $2.95

E479   GENET, JEAN / Letters to Roger Blin / $1.95

E577   GENET, JEAN / The Maids and Deathwatch: Two Plays / $2.95

E374   GENET, JEAN / The Screens / $1.95

E482   GOMBROWICZ, WITOLD / The Marriage / $1.95

E451   GOMBROWICZ, WITOLD / Ivona, Princess of Burgundia / $1.95

E484   GUARE, JOHN / Cop Out, Muzeeka,* Home Fires / $1.95 *[See also Showcase I: Plays from the O'Neill Foundation, John Lahr, ed. B233 / $1.95]

E615   HARRISON, PAUL CARTER (Ed.) / The Kuntu Drama / $4.95 (Kabnis by Jean Toomer, A Season in the Congo by Aime Cesaire, The Owl Answers and A Beast Story by Adrienne Kennedy, Great Goodness of Life by Imamu Amiri Baraka (LeRoi Jones), Devil Mas' by Lennox Brown, The Sty of the Blind Pig by Phillip Hayes Dean, Mars By Clay Goss, The Great MacDaddy by Paul Carter Harrison)

E457   HERBERT, JOHN / Fortune and Men's Eyes / $2.95

B154   HOCHHUTH, ROLF / The Deputy / $2.95

B200   HOCHHUTH, ROLF / Soldiers / $1.50

E427   HOFMANN, GERT / The Burgomaster / $1.50

E456   IONESCO, EUGENE / Exit the King / $2.95

E101   IONESCO, EUGENE / Four Plays (The Bald Soprano, The Lesson, The Chairs,* Jack, or The Submission) / $1.95 *[See also Eleven Short Plays of the Modern Theater, Samuel Moon, ed. B107 / $2.45]

E646   IONESCO, EUGENE / A Hell of a Mess / $3.95

E506   IONESCO, EUGENE / Hunger and Thirst and Other Plays / $1.95

E189   IONESCO, EUGENE / The Killer and Other Plays
        (Improvisation, or The Shepherd's Chameleon, Maid to
        Marry) / $2.45
E613   IONESCO, EUGENE / Killing Game / $1.95
E259   IONESCO, EUGENE / Rhinoceros* and Other Plays (The
        Leader, The Future is in Eggs, or It Takes All Sorts to Make
        a World) / $1.95 *[See also Seven Plays of the Modern
        Theater, Harold Clurman, ed. GT422 / $4.95]
E485   IONESCO, EUGENE / A Stroll in the Air and Frenzy for Two:
        Two Plays / $2.45
E119   IONESCO, EUGENE / Three Plays (Amédée, The New
        Tenant, Victims of Duty) / $2.95
E387   IONESCO, EUGENE / Notes and Counter Notes / $3.95
E496   JARRY, ALFRED / The Ubu Plays / $2.95
E443   JELLICOE, ANNE / Shelley, or The Idealist / $1.50
E633   LAHR, JOHN (Ed.) / Grove Press Modern Drama / $6.95
        (The Caucasian Chalk Circle by Bertolt Brecht, The Toilet
        by Imamu Amiri Baraka (LeRoi Jones), The White House
        Murder Case by Jules Feiffer, The Blacks by Jean Genet,
        Rhinoceros by Eugene Ionesco, Tango by Slawomir Mrozek)
B233   LAHR, JOHN (Ed.) / Showcase I: Plays from the Eugene
        O'Neill Foundation / $1.95 (Who's Happy Now by Oliver
        Hailey, The Indian Wants the Bronx by Israel Horovitz,
        Father Uxbridge Wants to Marry by Frank Gagliano,
        Muzeeka by John Guare)
E545   LAHR, JOHN / Up Against the Fourth Wall: Essays on
        Modern Theater / $2.95
B142   McCLURE, MICHAEL / The Beard / $1.25
B107   MOON, SAMUEL (Ed.) / One Act: Eleven Short Plays of the
        Modern Theater / $2.45 (Miss Julie by August Strindberg,
        Purgatory by William Butler Yeats, The Man With the
        Flower in His Mouth by Luigi Pirandello, Pullman Car
        Hiawatha by Thornton Wilder, Hello Out There by William
        Saroyan, 27 Wagons Full of Cotton by Tennessee Williams,
        Bedtime Story by Sean O'Casey, Cecile by Jean Anouilh,
        This Music Crept by Me Upon the Waters by Archibald
        MacLeish, A Memory of Two Mondays by Arthur Miller,
        The Chairs by Eugene Ionesco)

E410   MROZEK, SLAWOMIR / Six Plays: The Police, Out at Sea, Enchanted Night, The Party, Charlie, The Martyrdom of Peter Ohey / $2.45

E433   MROZEK, SLAWOMIR / Tango / $1.95

E568   MROZEK, SLAWOMIR / Vatzlav / $1.95

E462   NICHOLS, PETER / Joe Egg / $2.95

E650   NICHOLS, PETER / The National Health / $3.95

E393   ORTON, JOE / Entertaining Mr. Sloane / $2.95

E470   ORTON, JOE / Loot / $1.95

E567   ORTON, JOE / What The Butler Saw / $2.40

E583   OSBORNE, JOHN / Inadmissible Evidence / $2.45

B110   OSBORNE, JOHN / Plays for England and The World of Paul Slickey / $1.45 (The Blood of the Bambergs and Under Plain Cover)

B354   PINTER, HAROLD / Old Times / $1.95

E315   PINTER, HAROLD / The Birthday Party* and The Room: Two Plays / $1.95 *[See also Seven Plays of the Modern Theater, Harold Clurman, ed. GT422 / $4.95]

E299   PINTER, HAROLD / The Caretaker* and The Dumb Waiter: Two Plays / $1.95 *[See also Modern British Drama, Henry Popkin, ed. GT422 / $5.95]

E411   PINTER, HAROLD / The Homecoming / $1.95

E432   PINTER, HAROLD / The Lover, Tea Party, The Basement: Three Plays / $1.95

E480   PINTER, HAROLD / A Night Out, Night School, Revue Sketches: Early Plays / $1.95

GT614 POPKIN, HENRY (Ed.) / Modern British Drama / $5.95 (A Taste of Honey by Shelagh Delaney, The Hostage by Brendan Behan, Roots by Arnold Wesker, Serjeant Musgrave's Dance by John Arden, One Way Pendulum by N. F. Simpson, The Caretaker by Harold Pinter)

E538   ROSEWICZ, TADEUSZ / The Card Index and Other Plays / $1.95

E635   SHEPARD, SAM / The Tooth of Crime and Geography of a Horsedreamer / $3.95

E626   STOPPARD, TOM / Jumpers / $1.95

B319   STOPPARD, TOM / Rosencrantz and Guilderstern Are Dead / $1.95

E660   STOREY, DAVID / In Celebration / $2.95

B212   TUOTTI, JOSEPH D. / Big Time Buck White / $1.25
E434   VIAN, BORIS / The Generals' Tea Party / $1.95
E414   VIAN, BORIS / The Empire Builders / $2.95
E458   VIAN, BORIS / The Knacker's ABC / $1.95
E62   WALEY, ARTHUR (Translator) / The No Plays of Japan / $3.95
E519   WOOD, CHARLES / Dingo / $1.95

Critical Studies

E127   ARTAUD, ANTONIN / The Theater and Its Double / $2.95
GT423   BOWERS, FAUBIAN / Theatre in the East: A Survey of Asian Dance and Drama / $3.95
E520   COE, RICHARD N. (Ed.) / The Theater of Jean Genet: A Casebook / $3.95
E441   COHN, RUBY (Ed.) / Casebook on Waiting for Godot / $3.95
E479   GENET, JEAN / Letters to Roger Blin / $1.95
E387   IONESCO, EUGENE / Notes and Counter Notes / $3.95
E545   LAHR, JOHN / Up Against the Fourth Wall: Essays on Modern Theater / $2.95

Other Grove Press Paperbacks

☐ ALLEN, DONALD M., ed. *The New American Poetry.* E237/$3.95

☐ ARSAN, EMMANUELLE. *Emmanuelle.* B361/$1.95
      —Emmanuelle II. B383/$1.95

☐ BECKETT, SAMUEL. *Three Novels. Molloy; Malone Dies; The
      Unnamable.* B78/$1.95
      —Endgame. E96/$1.95
      — Waiting for Godot. E33/$1.95

☐ BERNE, ERIC, M.D. *Games People Play.* B186/$1.95
      *—A Layman's Guide to Psychiatry and
      Psychoanalysis.* B380/$1.95

☐ BRAUTIGAN, RICHARD. *A Confederate General from Big Sur.* B283/$1.50

☐ BRECHT, BERTOLT. *Galileo.* B120/$1.95
      —Mother Courage and Her Children. B108/$1.50

☐ BURROUGHS, WILLIAM S. *Naked Lunch.* B115/$1.95

☐ CUMMINGS, E. E. *100 Selected Poems.* E190/$1.95

☐ FANON, FRANTZ. *The Wretched of the Earth.* B342/$1.95

☐ GENET, JEAN. *The Balcony.* E130/$2.95

☐ IONESCO, EUGENE. *Four Plays. The Bald Soprano; The Lesson;
      The Chairs; Jack, or The Submission.* E101/$1.95

☐ KEROUAC, JACK. *The Subterraneans.* B300/$1.50

☐ LAWRENCE, D. H. *Lady Chatterley's Lover.* B9/$1.95

☐ MALCOLM X. *Autobiography of Malcolm X.* B146/$1.95

☐ MILLER, HENRY. *Tropic of Cancer.* B10/$1.95
      —Tropic of Capricorn. B59/$1.95

☐ PINTER, HAROLD. *The Homecoming.* E411/$1.95

☐ REAGE, PAULINE. *Story of O* (film ed.). B396/$1.95

☐ SCHUTZ, WILLIAM C. *Joy.* B323/$1.95

☐ SNOW, EDGAR. *Red Star Over China.* E618/$3.95

☐ STOPPARD, TOM. *Rosencrantz & Guildenstern Are Dead.* B319/$1.95
      —Travesties. E661/$1.95

☐ SUZUKI, D. T. *Introduction to Zen Buddhism.* B341/$1.95

☐ TRUFFAUT, FRANCOIS. *The Story of Adele H.* B395/$2.45

At your bookstore, or order below.

Grove Press, Inc., 196 West Houston St., New York, N.Y. 10014.

Please mail me the books checked above. I am enclosing $_____
(No COD. Add 35¢ per book for postage and handling.)

Name _____

Address _____

City_____State_____Zip_____